#MAMI

*An Experience in Motherhood,
Sisterhood & Daughterhood*

ANGIE FORD

#Mami: An Experience in Motherhood, Sisterhood & Daughterhood

Copyright © 2017 by Angie Ford

ISBN   978-0-9993650-0-7 (paperback)
         978-0-9993650-1-4 (hardcover)

Edited by:
Maritza Ford Johnson
Dr. Portia Ellis Carter
Luna F. Ramirez

Contributors:
Francella Ford
Maritza Ford Johnson
Yiniva Córdoba

Contents

Dedicated to:

My siblings (Francie and Maritza), aunts (Lois and Brenda), nephews (AJ and Jalen), Mami's godchildren (Tony, Xiomara, Karen, Edwin, Freddie, Tyra and Gisela) and her best friends (Neva and Yiniva). I want this to be a gift to all of you because of what you each meant to Mami.

In Loving Memory
OF
Jean Arial Ford Alleyne

November 3, 1935 – March 30, 2017

Introduction

GROWING UP I always knew that my Mother (#Mami) was a very special soul. She had unique qualities that were exemplified in the ways that she met and kept people around her. She had a way of making everyone feel special. Mami was the most beautiful soul that I ever met. Mami never compared us, she always encouraged and taught us how to survive in this world. I never really understood the impact Mami had in this world until she died on March 30th, 2017. I knew she was special, but after that dreadful day, I was filled with joy and comfort to hear the things that people who knew Mami well and those who barely knew her, were saying about her. Meaning that it did not take long for Mami to plant her seeds of wisdom and joy in the hearts of people that she met along her journey of life on this earth.

I have always been pretty good at expressing myself in writing. I find it therapeutic. I would typically write after taking a trip and feeling the need to describe my experience by including writing and my photographs to share with others. I quickly found that my photos and my words were impacting others. I shared them through my social media pages and my following became very solid and consistent. Therefore, I continued with this task. I then began sharing pictures of Mami and me, as she visited in Stone Mountain and when we traveled together. She became an instant sensation.

Any photograph of her on my pages would always get more "Likes" than anything that I ever posted. I loved it and she did too. The idea of writing this book actually came from a comment on my Facebook page from my cousin Luna F. Ramirez. She had been following my postings of Mami and she had experienced Mami also growing up in Panama. She is the daughter of my Dad's sister Dorothea. But, the commentary that followed and the inbox messages that were sent thereafter encouraging me to write the book, proved to be what I needed to get me going. I immediately discussed with my sisters and they both gave me the greenlight to proceed. I began jotting down ideas for chapters the following day and started making phone calls to key people in Mami's circle to let them know that I would be interviewing them. Everyone was so excited and thought it was a great idea and a great way to pay tribute to the unique, outstanding soul that Mami was. The title "#MAMI"came about because I would tag her pictures on Facebook to label any postings of Mami and the idea for the book came about via a social media suggestion.

For my sisters and me, our relationship with Mami was just the norm. Little did we know, what we had with Mami was not really the norm for the rest of the world. We assumed it was. Mother/daughter relationships can be so difficult for so many people and I am finding that out now. For us, it was smooth because Mami always found a balance to ensure that nobody felt left out or less than. She spread her love evenly across. I never felt like she loved me any more or less than my siblings. She didn't only do this with us. She did this with her godchildren, grandchildren, nieces/nephews, siblings, friends and even strangers. She had a way of connecting with people instantly and they seem to not be able to get enough of her. She was truly an angel on earth.

Mami was the best example of being a daughter, she took care of her mother (Abuela) and all the elders in our family, best example of a wife as she gave up working and became a full time housewife to care for us and was faithful to Papi until the end, best example of a mother as she cared for us and showed us equal love and not allowed us to feel any more or less than each other, best example of a sister as she is referred to as that best "big sister" anyone could ever ask for by her siblings, best example of a friend as she is called "best friend" by all of her girlfriends and best example of a Godmother, as she is adored by every single one of her godchildren. I must say that Mami was always that glue that held us together. Upon her death, we became even closer. I reconnected with her godchildren, her childhood friends, my childhood friends, my cousins and we now chat almost every day, thanks to technology. We send inspiring messages and we tell each other "I love you" more often. Mami once again is doing what she did best and that is keeping us connected and faithful. I hope that the following chapters will help anyone to forge great relationships with their mother, daughter and/ or friend. Relationships that will last a lifetime and be etched in your souls forever or maybe inspire you to write a book. I have to agree that writing this book has been therapeutic for me and helped me heal from my loss. Life is a gift from God and the way Mami lived life was a gift to anyone that came in contact with her on her journey on earth. For those that did not meet Mami personally, this is my gift to you. #MAMI has done it again.

Angie Ford
Stone Mountain, Georgia

Born on 3rd of November in Panama

O N NOVEMBER 3RD, 1903 with the support of the U.S. government, Panama issued a declaration of independence from Colombia. In 1903, the Hay-Herrán Treaty was signed with Colombia, granting the United States use of the Isthmus of Panama in exchange for financial compensation. The U.S. Senate ratified the treaty under leadership of President Theodore Roosevelt who gave the approval to the rebellion by Panamanian nationalists, which began on November 3, 1903. This was the beginning of sovereignty for the now Republic of Panama. From this day forth the 3rd of November is celebrated by Panamanians as one of the biggest holidays in the country. The day begins with the sounding of the "Dianas" by the Panamanian Firemen Force. I can still remember hearing them as I grew up and it still gives me goosebumps to hear them play so loud and proudly on that morning year after year.

Being born in Panama on the 3rd of November is like being born in the United States on the 4th of July. It is a celebration whether you want to have one or not. My Mother was born Jean Arial Alleyne on November 3rd, 1935 in Panama City, Panama to parents Castell Alleyne (GrandDaddy) and Mildred Alleyne (Abuela). Both parents were descendants of immigrants from the West Indies, who came to Panama for the building of the Canal. My GrandDaddy, worked for the Panama Canal Commission until he retired. My grandmother Mildred was a housewife. Overall, they did fairly well for themselves and provided for their children. My Mother was the third of six. She had a big brother, Tio Joe and four sisters, two of whom died. Ruth died from an illness and was born between Tio Joe and Mami and Abigail was stillborn between Mami and Tia Lois. My aunts Lois and Brenda were her younger siblings and she cared for them, like a mother. She was 10 years older than Lois and 13 years older than Brenda, also known as "Baby Doll".

As a child, Mami's birthday celebration was always done big. Her parents and neighbors would take her to see the parade at Palacio Legislativo. She and her friends would enjoy the parade and all the patriotic festivities. Abuela would dress her up and she would enjoy her day, as a celebrity. As an adolescent, this tradition continued, but now she and her friends would go out and celebrate on their own. Mami would have her dresses made and her shoes also because her feet were so small. Mami and her girlfriends would continue this tradition for many years to come prior to her getting married. When she met Papi, the celebration continued. It just seemed to get bigger as the years went by. The 3rd of November became Mami's Day for anyone that knew her. No invitation was required. Everyone in her circle knew exactly where and what they would be doing on that particular day of the year.

I remember growing up in Panama and looking forward to the excitement of the 3rd of November celebration. Not only for the parades throughout the city, but for the big celebration that followed at our home, thereafter. Seems like everyone knew that Mami's birthday was on that date. My friends, my sister's friend, family, teachers, neighbors, etc. all knew this tidbit of information. We did not have to invite anyone over. People just came to the house to celebrate Mami and I was always so proud to see how many would come. I was also very observant of how meticulously she would prepare for their arrival.

A typical 3rd of November morning began with us chanting and singing happy birthday to her, as she rushed to get us dressed and in our uniforms to head up to the school to salute the flag and participate in the yearly patriotic and civic rituals. One year, it began with us hiring some Mariachis to serenade her early morning. We woke up the entire neighborhood. But everyone enjoyed it and most people in Panama sleep very lightly on the eve of 3rd of November anyway. By the time I was in middle school, I participated in the parade in the city to salute the President of our Republic of Panama. Mami would put the TV on and watch the parade and wait to see our school come across the screen. She was so proud of her choice of education for us. November is considered rainy season in Panama and regardless of rain or shine, the parade went on. After it was over, we would return home and many friends will follow for the remainder of the day. Mami would have something quick for us to eat, as she continued to prepare for the "Big" celebration later on that same day. We would all engage in the preparation for the arrival of her guests. We would borrow chairs and tables from neighbors or the church and line them up in the garage area. But prior to setting up the chairs and tables, we would hose down the front porch and the garage flooring to make sure it was all clean. We would then proceed with any decorations in red, white and blue, (the colors in the Panamanian flag). The music would be playing in the background as a prelude to the upcoming celebration. This was the ritual for me during my entire childhood until I turned eighteen and decided to leave for college. But, the celebration continued without me and I hated to miss it.

I recall seeing Mami in the kitchen cooking food for an army and wondering if she was tired as she prepared. But, I never asked because I assumed that was something that she enjoyed doing. Now that I look back, I see where I get that same spirit of preparing for an event that I am hosting. The adrenaline of hosting your guests takes over and you want everyone to have a great time and enjoy the time they spend in your home. Regardless of the effort required to get it all together. The joy of knowing that your doors are open and people come to celebrate with you, far outweighs anything else. I know how she felt all those years because I learned from the best. My parents' home became "party central" at a very young age for us because of its centric location and spacious environment. One of Mami's best friends, Beverly, used to host her birthday party at my parent's home for many years and we loved seeing the adults dance and have a good time.

November 3rd, 1996, is etched in my mind because it was the last birthday Mami had with Papi. Papi had been diagnosed with colon cancer five years prior and battled hard via surgeries and chemotherapy. I remember living in New Jersey while all of this was going on for Papi. My best friend from high school, Marisol, stepped in and accompanied Mami during one of my Papi's surgeries and Mami was forever grateful to her for the support she gave her that day. But, that was a testimony of the strong relationships Mami had forged even with my friends. My Mami's home was like her home and my parents were like hers and this is how Marisol felt and she always expressed that to me. Marisol ate and spent the night at my home so much, she was like a permanent fixture for us. She continued to visit and hang around even after I left to the United States for college. Everyone in the neighborhood knew when I was home from college because her car was parked in our garage for days. In September of 1996, the doctors told us that there wasn't anything else they could do for Papi and it was just a matter of time. Therefore, I decided to head home to celebrate Mami's birthday with her and relieve her somewhat from caring for Papi. I remember that birthday morning so vividly. Papi had not been able to eat much and everything he ate would not stay down. But on that 3rd of November, he woke up and got out of bed and asked for bacon and eggs. I was surprised, as everyone else in the household. He came down the stairs and ate at the table with Mami and my big sister Francie. The smile on Mami's face was priceless. My Papi knew what November 3rd was supposed to be like and he made it happen for her, at least for a few hours. As expected, he was not able to hold the food down. But he tried in an effort to celebrate her. He also participated in all the festivities to follow. He wanted us to proceed with our yearly ritual on her birthday. Overall the day went well, given the circumstances. The crowd arrived and we all enjoyed the party and seeing Papi involved. It was Mami's day and it showed on her face. As I prepared to depart, I told Papi that my baby sister Maritza will be visiting soon. A few weeks later, Maritza and her now husband Alan came to Panama to visit Papi for the last time. He passed away on December 4, 1996. We were so glad that we came back home when we did to say our goodbyes and celebrate Mami at the same time.

Maritza and Alan proceeded to get married on June 20th, 1998 in Montego Bay, Jamaica. We planned for a year expecting to just have a few people show up. Well, we had sixty five family members and friends show up. There was a delegation from Panama of twenty people that came on COPA airlines. They even made the newspaper as a group traveling for a wedding. My Mami's friends, neighbors, and family felt the need to come and support her and my sister during this event. This was her first child to walk down the aisle and Mami was going to be the one to walk her down that aisle. We debated as sisters about who would be the best choice to step into Papi's shoes for this event and it did not take long to come to the conclusion that Mami was the only choice. Mami had just had a lump removed from her breast and was nursing a wound while she traveled. I remember helping her get dressed to ensure her dress did not irritate her wound or get soiled. We all wanted her to look perfect as she gave my sister away. Mami had lost so much weight from the stress of caring for my Papi and we were concerned for her. She had not taken good care of herself during those five years of his battle with cancer. Later on during that same year (1998), Mami was diagnosed with osteoporosis and requiring a hip replacement. Therefore, we scheduled the surgery and made arrangements for my Tio Joe to come from NYC to care for her and Abuela. Abuela was blind and this was her first born, which she had not seen or heard from in a while. Therefore, we made it happen and he was there for her surgery to care for both his mother and sister. It was his pleasure to do so. These two women had been his backbone his entire life and stood by him through thick and thin. My sister Maritza and I decided to surprise the entire family by showing up for 3rd of November that year to celebrate Mami's birthday. The entire crew that went to Jamaica with us for the wedding knew we were coming and kept the secret. Mami came to the door with her walker and was nothing but smiles when she saw us. We did what we did best and that was celebrate Mami, once again. After the wedding in Jamaica we gave all our guests & family members a t-shirt as a thank you token for making the trip. The Panama crew all wore their t-shirts for the birthday celebration that year and we relived the wedding event all over again.

I decided to move to Stone Mountain, Georgia in 1999 from Plainfield, New Jersey and build a home. My home was completed in September of that year. By November Mami and Abuela were there to visit. So we celebrated Mami's birthday in my new home. I called my cousin Mireya and she called some other Panamanian friends to come over, as well as some of my new friends in Georgia. We celebrated Mami's birthday and made sure she had cake and ice cream. November 3rd, will always be celebration day for Panamanians. But for us it will forever be Mami's birthday.

Mami moved to the United States as a permanent resident in May of 2009 after Abuela died in April of 2008. Mami's new home was with my baby sister Maritza in Indianapolis and although the celebrations became much smaller, we still celebrated and her phone rang all day long from near and far. Our family and friends just wanted her to know that she was still remembered and special. With technology, we streamed the parade on the television or laptop for her to feel at home. She kept the phone close by to answer all her phone calls. Mami made new friends while living in Indianapolis, so now they came over to celebrate her. I would travel to Indianapolis, as often as I could to celebrate with her.

For Mami's 75th birthday in 2010, we decided to return to her birthplace to celebrate one more time with friends and family. Unfortunately, my baby sister Maritza and her family could not join us due to the kid's school schedule. I traveled back to Panama on October 30th, 2010 with enough time to get the festivities organized and planned. My cousin Tamara and big sister Francie assisted me remotely prior to my arrival with ordering the tamales and food. When I got there, I arranged for the DJ equipment. My cousins Ricky and Marcella joined me in Panama from Brooklyn for this celebration. It was a milestone birthday and needed to be done big. The neighbors were ready and excited to be a part of this. I contacted my childhood and high school friends and they all said they were in. Since it is a holiday every year, it was easy to get people to participate. The day prior we cleaned up the garage area and began moving furniture around. The day of the party, we decorated, picked up the food, set up the music and the projector for a special presentation. The party was in full swing by 7PM. The guests began arriving right at 6PM. We danced the night away and caught up with old friends. We sang happy birthday to the top of our lungs. Seemed like the entire neighborhood was with us that day. I had a video presentation for Mami with pictures we had taken over the years and the background music was the song "A Song for Mama" by Boyz to Men. The last clip from the video was a message from my baby sister Maritza, Alan and the grandkids wishing her a happy 75th birthday. I could see the emotion in her eyes, as she watched it play. We ate ice cream and cake and return to dancing and drinking the night away. November 4th is also a holiday in Panama. Therefore, there wasn't any rush to end the party. That was the last birthday celebration that she had in her birthplace and it was one to remember.

In early 2015, I asked Mami what she wanted to do for her 80th birthday and she said she did not want a party because she had that her entire life. So, I suggested a trip and suggested Rome to go see the Vatican and the Pope. Mami was a devout Catholic and this was probably the best gift we could have ever given her. I was on the phone with her when I suggested the trip and I could feel her excitement bursting through the phone. Therefore, I spoke to my sisters and made sure they could take the time off. I wanted this to be a trip for Mami and her daughters only. We had not traveled all together as mother/daughters since I had left for college in 1985. She traveled with us individually, but not all four of us like we did for our summer vacations during our childhood. I started planning the trip and saving my frequent flyer miles. I looked for hotels close by the Vatican because I did not want to have to walk too far, knowing that Mami had a knee issue. Originally, I had the trip scheduled for end of September. I chose to take her early because I wanted to take advantage of the fall weather in Europe and also needed to ensure she was back home for the 3rd of November to take her phone calls. This was the big "80" and of course her phone was going to ring off the hook. So being out of the country was not an option. Those phone calls were priceless and we had to safeguard them. Mami needed to be reachable on that day. On a Sunday evening in July, Mami called me to say that she was reading the church bulletin and she proceeded to inform me that the Pope was going to be on tour in Cuba and the United States at the end of September. Exactly the same week that we had planned to go to

Rome. I laughed and said, I guess this is your way of telling me we need to change the dates and she just laughed too. Mami was so into her faith that she knew the Pope's schedule and we found that hilarious. So I had to scramble to rearrange the dates and push it out for another week and I made sure that he was going to be in Rome that week. Granted, there was no guarantee we would see the Pope while there. But, just knowing he was behind one of those doors made her feel better. Mami and Maritza met Francie and I in Atlanta to board our overnight flight into Rome. As we got on the plane I handed a note to the flight attendant telling her the reason for our trip and her seat number. When the plane reached cruising altitude, the flight attendant proceeded to announce her name and the reason for her trip and her seat number. The entire plane bursted out in applause and she was so excited and the passengers in the surrounding area all acknowledged her and made her feel special. Her eyes lit up like a child at Christmas and that brought all of us so much joy. This was her birthday gift and all of her daughters were there to celebrate with her. On her actual birthday that year, I traveled to Indianapolis to celebrate with her. We had her friend Clara and the Carrolls over at the house and we sang happy birthday, ate cake and ice cream and watched her enjoy all of her phone calls. My gift to her was a photo book from our trip to Rome. A book that she treasured and showed to everyone that came to visit. I remember standing at her bedroom door once, as she sat on her bed and looked through her photo book for the umpteenth time and all she could do was smile. I could only imagine what she was thinking. At that moment, I knew we had made the right choice in taking her to Rome for her 80th, 3rd of November in 2015. Because it was a year to remember!

"The two most important days in your life are the day you are born and the day you find out why"

– MARK TWAIN

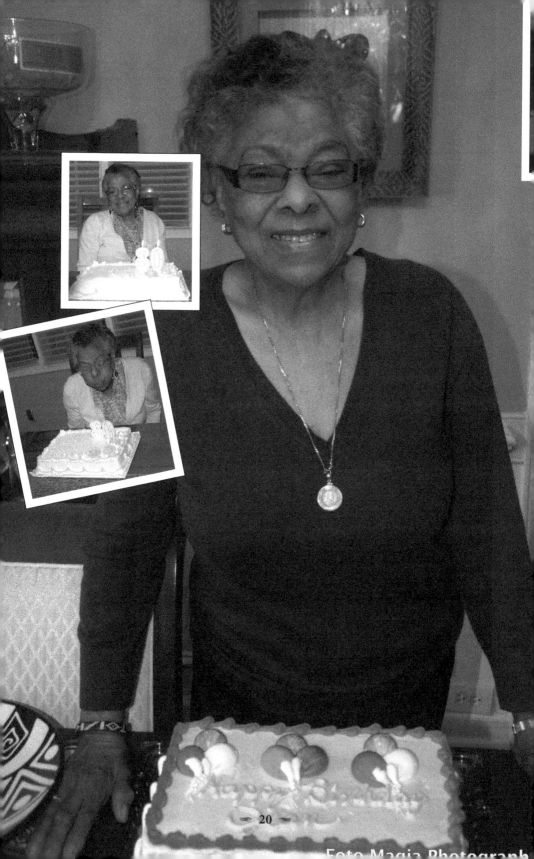

20

Motherhood

"**M**OTHERHOOD" TRANSLATED TO Spanish is "Maternidad". The dictionary defines it as state of being a Mother. Such a vague description of what it really means. I think every daughter or son with a good or fair relationship would define "Motherhood" by placing a picture of their mother into the dictionary. I know that I would define as such. For me "Motherhood" equals "Mami" and for my sisters and me, "Mami" equals "Jean Arial Ford Alleyne". Becoming a mother was Mami's biggest joy and our biggest blessing for life to have her as our "Mami". This word "Mami" just rolls off our tongues like no other. Growing up, it was "Mami this" and "Mami that". But, Mami never got tired of us calling her name. Well at least she never showed it. She knew she was responsible for us and she served us well.

Mami experienced motherhood for the first time on August 25th, 1963 when Francie was born. She was a big baby with a head full of hair. She had chubby cheeks and was adored by everyone. She is the first born and that in itself makes her unique for life. Mami and Papi paraded Francie around to family and friends. They took her to the fair, zoo and carnival parades. Mami would make her costumes for carnival and dress her up. When Francie was enrolled in kindergarten she was the tallest of all the kids. She is still the tallest of all of us.

According to Mami's close friends, she was so excited with her first child. She ate a pint of ice cream almost every night during her first pregnancy and Papi would bring it for her. Mami's sister/friend, Yiniva, which I will tell you more about later on, would stay with Mami after work during her pregnancy until Papi would get home. Francie was named after Papi's mother, Francella. Papi actually named all of us. My name "Angelica", he chose because he liked an actress named Angelica Maria at the time. My baby sister Maritza was actually named by Francie. Her name came from a television personality that hosted the Christmas toy show. Her name was Maritza Morales and Francie was fascinated with her. So Mami really did not have much of a say so in our names. Mami chose her dear friend and co-worker Yiniva to be Francie's Godmother. Yiniva was thrilled about this and returned the honor when she had her first child. She asked Mami to be her Godmother. Both Yiniva and Mami took being godparents very seriously. Yiniva has served Francie extremely well. She is also my confirmation Godmother. I am told that with the arrival of Francie, holidays became so exciting in my parents and grandparents household. Mami's parents lived on the Canal Zone at the time and they cared for Francie while my parents went to work. They spoiled her as much as Mami and Papi did. Francie was the first grandchild.

Three years later on August 12th, 1966, I was born. By now Mami had perfected her motherhood skills. She knew exactly what to do. Francie took possession of me and called me her "Baby". She would tell everyone "that's my baby". No one could touch me. She would sit me up amongst her dolls and treat me as one. My parents were living in an apartment building on Via Porras in the San Francisco neighborhood in Panama City, Panama. I was welcomed with open arms. I was planned for. I did not have the head full of hair like Francie, but I had big eyes and long legs. Everyone thought I would be taller than I am today at 5 feet 3 inches. I gave Mami a run for her money. I was active and mischievous. I would not stay still. Mami told me that she and Papi once went to the supermarket and they had me in the cart. I was just a baby. At that time, wigs were very popular. So Mami had one on and it was red, short and very chic. Mami said I kept looking at her strange, as if I did not know who she was. Mami then took me out of the cart to hand me to Papi and I latched on to her wig and would not let go. She said I wanted to take that darn wig off. Mami said the struggle was real as she handed me off to Papi. Papi was cracking up laughing after she finally got me to let go of the wig and she adjusted it on to her head. I still crack up laughing when I think of this incident and try to picture the scene. Mami learned my patterns and she mastered me. She figured that if I was too quiet, I was either sick or doing something I was not supposed to be doing. I was a Daddy's girl so I watched Papi's every move. One day, I decide to shave like Papi and I was quietly in their bathroom foaming my face and hairline. Mami knew I was not sick and I was quiet which meant I was doing something I was not supposed to. She came looking for me, as I put the razor to my hairline. She scared me and I cut a chunk of my hair out. The next thing Mami said was, "you are going to school like that tomorrow". I started to cry and she made believe I would be going like that. I cried all night. Next morning she combed my hair, pulled it back in a ponytail and went to her cosmetic bag, pulled out her eyeliner and colored my hairline in. I smiled as she did it. She was my Mami and she was not going to let me go out like that. She did this for about a week, as it grew back. She explained to me how dangerous that razor was and that I could have really hurt myself.

I was the athlete in the family and I went from one sport to another. Mami supported whatever sport I wanted to play. I asked Papi to get me a volleyball and knee pads. He got the volleyball, but forgot the knee pads. Therefore, I decided to find something that would pad my knees and I went into Mami's personal closet and found her sanitary napkins. They were "Kotex" brand, which was the most popular brand back then. They were big and bulky, with the long strap that went around the waist belt. I took two of them out and tied them around my knees. I had these big white bows on the back of my knees. They looked pretty to me. I was ready to go outside and show off my new volleyball and knee pads and I did. As we were playing on the basketball court, my GrandDaddy saw me. Unfortunately, he had had a stroke and lost his speech. But, he would sit on the balcony and watch us play. Well, he kept trying to get my attention and was looking like he was about to have another stroke. I paid no attention to him and kept playing and he went inside. Next thing I know, I felt Mami's breath behind my neck. She snatched me and pull the pads off. She punished me and told me not to ever go in her personal closet again. She later on explained the usage of the pads and asked Papi to please bring those knee pads that I had requested. Mami never punished without teaching the lesson. She made sure we understood our actions and consequences. She also kept her word. If she said, "wait until we get home", you knew something was going to happen. Mami did not play!

At one point, I thought Mami had played Major League Baseball because her aim was so perfect. I also thought Mami was the "Bionic Woman" because she heard everything, even if you whispered it under your breath. She also seemed to see everything. If Mami spoke and you did not get to moving in her timeframe the next thing you would see flying at you was whatever she could get her hands on. It could be a shoe, spoon, pot, etc. It also seemed to go around corners to get to you. We developed a skill of dodging, which worked well when we played dodge ball with the other kids. Mami disciplined us with love and we knew it and we turned out just fine.

By October 20th, 1969, when Maritza arrived, Mami had this motherhood thing down packed. Although, she was expecting a boy and the baby shower had everything green. Mami and Papi already had two girls and they really wanted that little boy. But, God blessed them with a very light skinned and red headed baby. She was beautiful and I remember playing with her. Francie now had a new baby and I was old news to her. But, I also had my own baby for the first time. I would play my little guitar for Maritza to get her to stop crying. Until this date, I still feel the need to protect Maritza like I did when we were kids. I was always ready to fight anyone who would tease her because she was a little chunky and kids could be mean at times. Maritza was the most sensitive one all of us. Her feelings got hurt easily and she cried easily. Mami would come rushing to see who was doing what to her. Of course, I always got the blame. But, Mami always knew who did what. She knew us very well. I remember an incident where I had done something and I let Maritza take the fall for it with Papi because I knew she would not get in trouble because she was the baby. Mami later on came to me and said that she knew that I did it and it was not nice for me to have let Maritza take the blame for what I had done.

Seven months after Maritza was born, we moved into the home that Papi and GrandDaddy built. It was huge and was our home until we sold it in 2011. We grew up in this home and Mami created so many memories for us. Mami had a green thumb and she planted beautiful flowers and trees all over the yard. We had a palm tree with coconuts, a papaya tree, a lime tree and several pepper plants. We had beautiful flowers that stayed in bloom. But, Mami cherished her roses. They were her favorites. Mami once planted a pineapple and we were amazed to see how it grew. Mami would stand and water her plants with the hose every evening. She diligently cared for her yard and it was beautiful. Mami was an animal lover and we had many dogs growing up. They were part of our family. She also had a parrot, "Lola", which she adored. Between the dogs and the parrot, the house was always filled with lots of life.

Mami loved photography. She took pictures of us from day one. She created a photo album for each of us and kept it up. It had in it, newborn, school, travel, carnival pictures, etc. Francie's album was red, mine was green and Maritza's was yellow. Maritza was the first to have an album with the plastic cover to protect the photographs. Our albums were made from paper pages, which would not make it over time. Mami handed each of us our albums, as we left home. I was the first to leave to go to college in New Orleans. I took mine with me and over the years the pages fell apart and I took the photos out and put them into a wooden box with the word "Memories" carved on the top of it. I cherished these memories. I had an amazing childhood in Panama and I wanted to keep that safe. In these days since everything is digital, I would suggest that instead of an album or scrapbook, that a parent should create an email account for each child and send pictures and love notes to that child. When the child becomes a teenager, hand over the account and password for them to read all the emails sent over the years. I think that email account would be a treasure box for that child and they will appreciate it for many years to come.

I think I got my love for photography from Mami. She was a fairly good photographer. She had a Polaroid Instamatic and she would take the pictures and hand them to me to fan them and watch them develop right before my eyes. She also had several Kodak cameras that required film and would get the film developed immediately. She had the type of cameras that had the cube flashes. I would play with the cameras and waste her film and she would let me. In college I took a class to learn to develop black and white. I then became a photographer for the yearbook and did very well. I had a Ricoh camera that I borrowed from my Tia Lois.

Motherhood meant everything to Mami. She quit her job to ensure our wellbeing. She wanted to be home to meet us at the door when we got off the school bus and make sure dinner was ready for us. She wanted to do homework with us. She did all these things to ensure we had a stable and prosperous childhood. Mami cooked, cleaned, washed clothes, combed hair, etc. She did it all for us. She had a dinner bell that she rang for us to know dinner was ready. Everybody in the neighborhood knew that sound of the bell and word would get to us wherever we were that Mami was ringing the bell. My friends and I would come running home and Mami would count heads and serve plates. It did not matter how many neighborhood kids I brought home. Mami fed us all. But, not before saying our grace. When we did have a chance to sit at the table with Mami to eat, she would always add one last phrase to her grace. Mami would always ask God to ensure that her "families" in the United States had food on their tables every day also.

As we got older and more independent, Mami had to find other things to do to entertain herself. So she took up learning how to make ceramics. Mami filled the house with her creations and she gave some out as gifts. It seemed like there was a piece of ceramic in every corner of the house. Mami loved her classes. She also attempted driving lessons, but those did not turn out too well. I did much better than her and told her not to worry that I would drive her around and I did, when I got my driver's permit.

While I was in college, Mami was diagnosed with uterine cancer. At the time I did not know how serious this was. But, she beat it! Mami was determined to not leave her girls motherless. She had a complete hysterectomy and radiation therapy. When I returned home for the summer break, I recall seeing her burn scars from the radiation therapy. Mami fought for us. She wanted to be there to see us graduate from college and just see us grow up. She told one of her friends that she prayed so much to God to allow her that opportunity and He granted her wish. The survival rate for that type of cancer is approximately 82%, as long as it has not metastasized. But, Mami had more work to do on this earth and only God determined what would happen next. Mami became a cancer survivor and she shared her story with many, including some of my dear friends.

Another role that Mami played during her motherhood and played it very well was of Santa Claus. Mami had hiding places throughout the house where she would hide the toys, as they bought them. Mami and my Godmother Neva did Christmas shopping together. By the time I figured out that Mami was Santa Claus, I had also figured out the hiding places. Unfortunately, I was the one to tell my baby sister Maritza that Mami was Santa. Of course, at first she did not believe me. Mami was so upset with me for ruining it for Maritza. Our bedrooms had an opening at the top for ventilation and we had bunk beds. I shared a room with Maritza and I slept on the top bed. On this particular Christmas Eve, I heard when my parents got up to put the toys under the tree. I looked over the overhang in my bedroom and watched them go up and down the stairs like little ants working through the night. As soon as they were done, I jumped down and told Maritza that Santa had arrived and she was sleepy and groggy, so she questioned how did I know? My response was "I saw him". I did not lie, I did see him or them. We jumped up and went downstairs to find everything on our Christmas list, as usual. Mami always told us that if we behaved and did well in school that Santa would reward us and she did just that because we all did extremely well in school. The company that Papi managed sold all sorts of sporting equipment and tires. So we got a new bike almost every year. This particular holiday season, I got sick at school and Mami had to go get me and bring me back home. Papi did not know that, so he sent his guys to deliver the bikes to the house for Mami to put into the secret room. A mysterious room in the house that had a lock and key and we could not go into around the holidays. I wonder why. Well my eyes got really big when I saw the delivery and Mami tried to send me upstairs to my room. But, I knew what was up and I could not wait to tell the rest when they got home. As soon as I heard the school bus arrive, I ran downstairs and waited at the door. I was ready to open my big mouth when I felt Mami's hand slap me on the back of my head and told me to shut up. Maritza had this puzzled look on her face and kept asking "what?" and I could not move or open my mouth. Mami knew I was going to tell. So she prepared for that moment and was able to avoid me spoiling it. I also knew I could never tell, thereafter because I was going to be in much trouble and may not get my bike. So I kept the secret until Christmas day.

Christmas of 2016 was our last Christmas with Mami, we didn't know it would be the last time. It was an amazing one, as usual. Christmas was always one of Mami's favorite holidays. During this last one we showered Mami with great gifts. One particular gift that got her surprised and had her eyes popping out of her face like a child, was an easel. Mami was always a good artist. She had started sketching to entertain herself. She took lessons from Bob Ross on his television show. So we got her art supplies for her to enjoy herself and have something to do during the day. When she opened the bag with the easel and the art supplies, she gasped from excitement. I knew then we had gotten her something that she wanted. It was never hard to please Mami. She appreciated whatever we gave her.

My childhood was an amazing one. It was filled with lessons and great memories that I still recall until this day. It was only possible because Mami took her "Motherhood" role super seriously and was determined to be the best mother possible. I must say that she did an excellent job. Mami treated us as equals. She figured out a way to spread her love across to ensure that no one felt left out. She allowed each of us to be individuals and different. She provided us with the tools necessary to make it in this world. Mami was only five feet tall, but growing up with her she looked like a giant. We had much respect for her and looked forward to her advice. As we became older she became more than our Mother. She was also our friend and we had the best of both worlds.

Mami's motherhood extended beyond her biological children. Mami was a mother to others also. My cousin Tamara is the daughter of Papi's youngest brother Noel. He died many years prior to Papi. When Noel died, Papi stepped into the father role for Tamara and Mami rolled right in with him. Tamara has a mother and is very close to her. But, Mami served as that second opinion that she could turn to. As Tamara got older and we had left for college, Mami extended her home to her after Tamara decided to leave her husband. She lived with Mami and Papi for some months until she got herself together to be on her own. Mami and Tamara got so close that Mami also confided in her. Tamara is more like a sister to us than a cousin because of the closeness she shared with Mami. When I asked Tamara how would she described Mami, she said "she was the best person she had ever met and was her second mother". Those words brought a smile to my face and gave me comfort and pride. I also asked her what did she miss the most about Mami and she said her Sunday phone calls. Mami would make her round of calls on Sundays after church. If Mami sensed that Tamara needed anything, she would immediately let us know. Mami knew Tamara was not going to ask her. But, Mami knew her other child too. In fact, Mami called some of our friends to check on them and we had no idea she was doing that until they said to us that they missed her phone calls. But, that is what Mami did. She was a nurturer and if you came into her life, she made sure she provided you with love and care. Something that every human being needs and should get. Mami's motherhood went far beyond us and she still gave us what we needed.

After Tamara, there was Mariluz and her kids. They also took up residence in Mami's home for a while until things got better for them and could be on their own. Mariluz was a friend of the family. Her brother dated my oldest sister Francie back in the day and we became close to their family. Mariluz took a liking to Mami, as everyone else and kept in touch with her. Mami was also very fond of her and treated her like a daughter. So when Mariluz needed a place to stay, Mami offered and we had no problem with it because we were in college in a different country and it gave Mami some company and someone to care and nurture. Mariluz's kids loved Mami because she treated them like grandchildren that she did not yet have. The kids were well mannered and very quiet. They have grown in very smart young men and always looked forward to seeing Mami when she returned to Panama to visit. They also took Mami's death very hard.

Being a mother is probably the hardest job on earth and it comes without instructions. You need faith, confidence, love, patience, family support, strong parenting partnership and many other qualities to do the job. It is easier if not done alone and thank God that Mami had Papi and her parents to support her during our crucial childhood years. She didn't only have her family, she also had a strong circle of friends that have been there for us and continue to be. My sisters and I are very fortunate to have experienced "Motherhood" via Mami. ***#Motherhood #Mami***

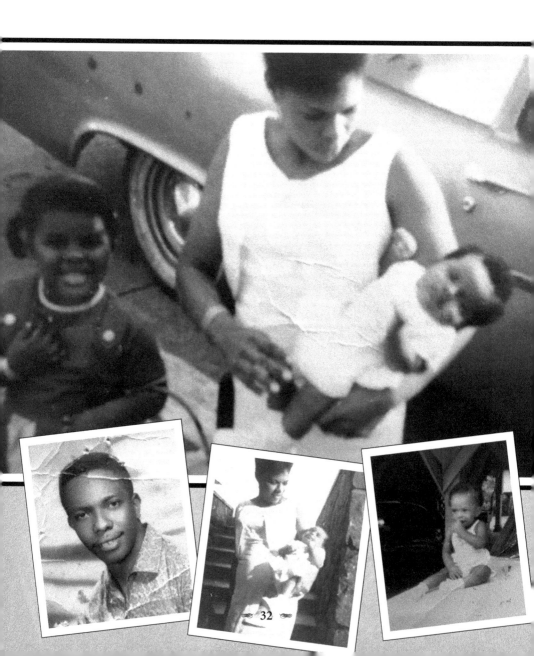

34

Our Education

AMI'S LOVE FOR education began at an early age. Abuela made sure that Mami was educated and enrolled in the right school. She attended elementary school at Republica de Chile School when they lived in Panama City. Because my GrandDaddy worked for the Canal Zone he was able to get quarters on the Canal Zone. Mami was moved from the city, to Red Tank, La Boca and then Pedro Miguel. Mami then attended the La Boca High School and graduated from there.

Enrolling us in one of the best schools in the nation was a top priority for Mami. The Instituto Episcopal San Cristobal, a twelve year, private school had just been in operation for a few years when Mami enrolled Francie and then me and Maritza. We attended IESC for twelve years, from first grade until twelfth grade. Our school was bilingual, which was very important to Mami because she knew that would open opportunities for us, as we graduated and entered the working world. She was right because at that time the best paying jobs were on the Canal Zone, which was United States territory and English was a requirement. We went to school in Spanish for one half of the day and the other half in English. We learned the English language very well. We speak and write it very proficiently. As you can see, my English background has served me well enough to write this book. Also my sister Francie worked for many years as an English-Spanish translator and still continues to do some translations projects.

When Mami was younger she wanted to be a nurse, but she let others discourage her and scare her about what a nurse would actually do. She was told that nurses would have to sleep with dead bodies and that scared her. So she went to seamstress and business administration school. She became a secretary and was excellent at typing and accounting. She worked at the same company my Papi worked at until she decided to quit in order to become a full-time housewife to ensure that our education was a priority.

At our school, we were known as "Hermanitas Ford" meaning the "Ford Sisters". Mami was very actively involved in the curriculum and ensuring we got what she was paying for. She paid for our tuition in full for a year during registration. She got a discount for paying in advance and she did. Getting that discount was a big deal to Mami because at one point she had all three of us at the same school. I recall Mami coming up to the school on several occasion when we complained to her about anything related to a teacher or the curriculum. She was known at the school. The administrators would say "here comes Mrs. Ford". But, at the same time they knew that she would not come up there unless there was a real problem. They respected her opinion and her feedback.

I remember whenever we had group projects at school that my classmates always wanted to be on my team because they knew that my team would meet at my home and Mami was going to make her famous Chow-Mein. Mami was a great cook and could whip up a meal quickly. On many occasions, I would just show up with friends without calling. We didn't have cell phones back then, and she would just get going, as soon as we arrived, to ensure we had something to eat. My classmate Dianitza, until this day still remembers Mami's Chow Mein and we still reminisce about those days at our home in Panama. Mami would also allow me to host my class parties at our home. We had a spacious garage or carport and I was into music and built speakers. I thought I was a DJ back then and my friends did too. So it was the party house. She was ok with us having our parties there because she knew we were good students and it did not interfere with our studies.

My sisters and I all graduated from IESC after our twelve year attendance. Mami was so proud to see each one of us walk across that stage. I could see the joy in her eyes and knew that she felt like she had accomplished part of her goal. The other part was to get us to college and really get us to be first generation college graduates in the family. My big sister Francie started college in Panama and chose to remain in the country. When I graduated, I was fortunate enough to get a full basketball scholarship to Xavier University in New Orleans. I was excited. My SAT scores were extremely high and allowed me not to require remedial courses. I went straight into my curriculum classes. I chose the Mathematics-Computer Science major. It was a dual degree. Throughout my high school years, I had always said I wanted to be an architect because I was really good at drawing and had a photographic memory. I had the best Mathematics teacher, Mr. Cornejo. He saw something in me that I did not recognize. Math was easy to me. He would enroll me into a national Math contest every year and it meant having to give up my Saturdays to practice with him. So, my senior year I decided to not do so well on my tests in an effort to discourage him from selecting me for the Math contest. He read straight through me and told me I was going anyway. I went along and participated, I did not win. But, I now cherish that experience. After I graduated from high school he called me and asked that I take a summer school course in computer science programming. I thought he had lost his mind. I had already graduated and was enjoying my summer. But, Mami encouraged me to go and I went. He taught me how to program in Basic language on a Commodore 64 computer and that was my first experience with a computer. I fell in love with programming and decided to major in it at Xavier University. I am still working in Computer Science and have made a living from it since I left college in December, 1988. Mami came to my college graduation and I could see how proud she was of me. I knew that I had made her proud. She supported me financially throughout my college years with my extracurricular expenses because my tuition and room/board was covered by my scholarship. I knew then, that I needed to support myself by getting a good job and I did. I had a job lined up from my summer internship experience. My company also paid for me to get my Masters in Computer Science in my first year as an employee. I went to Howard University in Washington, DC. At that time the company had a program that would allow me to go to school full time and reduce my salary, as long as I completed my program within a year and I did. They paid for all my books and with my reduced salary I took care of my living expenses. When I returned, they increased my salary according to the going rate and began my career as an engineer specializing in the telecommunication industry. In fact, twenty nine years later and I still work for the same company.

Before I graduated from Xavier, my baby sister Maritza decided to follow in my footsteps. My senior year overlapped with her freshman year in college. She applied and got accepted into the Psychology program. She applied and received financial aid to pay for tuition. Papi and Mami took out loans to support her also. Maritza went on to get her degree in four years, as scheduled. She then proceeded to go to nursing school at Dillard University and she finished at Loyola University in Chicago when she moved there. This was a dream come true for Mami because she wanted to be a nurse. So to see Maritza accomplish it was enough for her. Maritza then went on to get her Nurse Practitioner's degree and Mami was present for that also. I watched the joy on Mami's face that day that Maritza received her NP degree and receive it with honors. We celebrated her major accomplishment and Mami called and told everyone about it. Mami lived with Maritza at this point, so she indulged in watching her grow as a professional in her field of choice. Maritza is an awesome nurse. She specializes in geriatrics and cared for Mami until the end.

My big sister Francie was the last to decide to also attend Xavier University. She applied and got a music scholarship. Francie had always been musically inclined and very good at playing instruments. Mami enrolled Francie in guitar lessons at a very early age. Francie would practice at night and torture us until we complained and Mami would come out from her bedroom and ask her to go to bed and resume her practicing the following day. Francie went ahead and got a degree in music and education from Xavier University also. That completed Mami's dreams of all her daughters getting a college degree. She would proudly speak of each one of us to her family and friends. We all knew that Mami wanted the best for all of us and would sacrifice herself for us to obtain it. So we made her proud by becoming responsible citizens with jobs that pay taxes. We have gone on to have homes and vehicles of our own and treated Mami like a queen while she was here on earth with us. We gave back to Mami what she had given to us to allow us to be who we are today. We gave her peace of mind that we would be fine. Her job was done and well done. We made sure she knew that before she departed. We plan to continue honoring Mami's wishes by encouraging our next generations to finish high school and attend college. I already see Mami's education influence in what my baby sister Maritza is doing with her sons. They attended public school through middle school. Although it was a public school, it was a Spanish immersion program school where they learned to speak and write Spanish fluently. But, for high school she has enrolled them into Cathedral High School, a prestigious Catholic school in Indianapolis. The quality of education at this school is superb and we see the difference. They are prepared to make it into college with flying colors. My eldest nephew is currently a junior at Cathedral and has a 3.8 GPA. We are so proud of him and the youngest one has been accepted to begin his freshman year in the fall of 2017. I myself stay on top of the education of each of my godchildren and nephews too. With my nephews, they get five dollars for each 'A' they get on their report card. One of my first questions to my godchildren when I see or speak to them, is how is school going? I also share my story of how I got my scholarship all the way from Panama and went to school for free. I stress the importance of having great grades to be eligible for a scholarship. Graduating from college debt free makes a big difference. Education is definitely the key to success in life and Mami taught us that. *#Education*

40

Francella A. Ford Alleyne

41

Her Faith

THE DICTIONARY DEFINES "faith" as strong belief in God or in the doctrines of a religion, based on spiritual apprehension rather than proof. Mami had very strong faith. She lived as a devout Catholic for most of her life. Although, her first experiences with faith came from a different religion. Abuela was Baptist and Mami had a childhood friend named Gloria that took her to church and bible study and Mami read and learned the entire bible. Gloria was older than Mami and was a Seven Day Adventist. Gloria was a neighbor, her father was German. I recall that tidbit because Mami often mentioned it. Mami would always recall that experience with us and I found it amazing how she was so drawn to learn about God and Christ at such an early age. One thing I noticed about Mami a long time ago, was that she never knocked any other religions. Besides, the Jehovah Witness lady that came by the house once and she allowed her in and this lady began to knock her Catholic beliefs. Mami escorted her right back out and asked her not to come back. She was willing to hear about other faiths, but was not willing to have hers knocked down.

When Mami became a Catholic, back then mass was done in Latin and she learned Latin to be able to follow mass. For holy week she would put on the TV and follow the entire mass in Latin from the Vatican and understood everything. At one point, I thought she was talking in tongues until she explained to me what she was saying. Growing up in Panama and experiencing Holy week and Good Friday was a unique experience. Because Panama is predominantly Catholic country, that week is sacred. As of Thursday of that week, no liquor stores are open, no radio stations played any secular music, no one sells meat and as a child you were not allowed to go outside to play or create too much noise. On Good Friday, we would start off our day eating bun and cheese. This was a homemade "Holy Cross" bun, which one of our aunts or Mami would bake. Also on Good Friday we were told that we had to take a bath before noon otherwise, we would turn into a fish and we could not climb a tree, otherwise we would turn into monkeys. So many myths that to my knowledge are no longer in practice. At that time, we believed them. I remember going to the fish market to get our fish and shrimp to make dinner for that day. We did this year after year throughout my childhood. Mami and my Godmother Neva would always go to a play on that day at my school that depicted the resurrection of Christ. One year, when they went and left us at home, we decided to step outside and play baseball in the streets. The game was the girls against the boys. The game was so good because the girls were winning and it attracted a crowd from the apartment building across the street. We had neighbors cheering for us, as we beat the boys. This was unusual for a Good Friday. Remember it is a solemn day and we were not supposed to be outside. Well, when Mami came back home and saw the ruckus we were creating outdoors, the game quickly ended and we were grounded for the remainder of the weekend. Can't remember if we got Easter baskets that year.

Easter Sundays were a big deal growing up, Mami would make our outfits or buy them. She was a great seamstress. She went to school to learn how to sew and she was really good at it. I remember getting measured and watching her put together our outfits. She made our patterns from scratch using newspapers. She had a Singer sewing machine station and she loved it. She also made all the curtains for our home, which she switched out every holiday. On Easter morning, we always attended church and got dressed up. While looking through my childhood photo album, the one photo that always stands out is one of my Tio Joe and me for an Easter on the Canal Zone. He was stooped down with me and I had my Easter dress and my basket and he was just loving on me. I could tell from that photo that Easters were big in our family. This tradition was something that Mami passed along to us and my sister Maritza to her sons. The boys get dressed up every year for Easter and they all attend church as a family at St. Andrews Catholic Church in Indianapolis. Mami's funeral was the day after Easter Sunday in 2017. Of course, we got up that morning got dressed up and went to my church, Ray of Hope Christian Church in Decatur, Georgia. My Pastor, Cynthia Hale, knew of Mami's passing and she made sure to come over and meet my family and show us some love, as we prepared for the difficult following day.

Mami became a member of Iglesia de Piedra in Rio Abajo, Panama. She was an active member and we became members too. I made my first communion and confirmation at this church. We went to 7:30 a.m. mass every Sunday and sat in the same spot. We had a routine that we followed. After church, we would stop at the market to get lottery numbers and any ingredients required for her to make her Sunday dinner. For many years, my Papi would drive us to church and not go in. Then eventually, he started attending with us. I never asked Mami what brought on the change of heart. One funny thing happened to us on a Saturday afternoon. While Papi watched sports on TV, Mami, my sisters and I fell asleep for what we thought would be a short nap. When Mami got up it was 6:00 PM and for some reason she thought it was 6:00 AM on Sunday morning because it was already dark outside. She began to get dressed for church and we just followed. My Papi kept looking at us like we were crazy. Until he asked us where were we going and she told Papi that we were headed to church. He proceeded to explain that it was still Saturday and not Sunday morning. We all got a good laugh and went to get undressed. I remember laughing so hard with my parents and walking back to my room to take my itchy Sunday outfit off.

Mami's church began to grow in the community and we were proud members of it. We had extended family members and neighbors who also attended and we were always excited to see them after church. Mami belonged to a group called "Legion de Maria" translated is Legion of Mary. It was a group of women that gathered to say the rosary and spread God's message in the community. Mami was an "Auxiliary", she was responsible for saying the rosary daily for the "Legionnaire", the lead of the group. Her Legionnaire was a beautiful, tall lady named Maria Jose. Mami would host the meetings at her home weekly and she would prepare for the ladies all day long. I remember attending a few meetings and watching them talk about their next mission and study the bible. I was so proud of Mami because once again she was making a difference in her community.

Growing up Catholic in Panama allowed for many religious experiences. Mami took us to processions during Holy week, she took us to visit different historical churches like La Catedral, Iglesia del Carmen, Iglesia de San Jose (Golden Altar) and the Iglesia de San Felipe to see the Cristo Negro of Portobelo (the Black Christ of Portobelo). She gave us the history behind these churches, which have all become staples in Panama. I remember going to Portobelo as a child to see the Black Christ. I returned to Portobelo in April of 2016, for the first time since I was child and all the memories came right back as I entered the church. We also went to processions for Don Bosco and St. Jude. My Papi prayed to St. Jude often and had an altar at home dedicated to him. Papi's faith was strengthened due to Mami's. She encouraged him to go to church and by the time Papi got sick with cancer his faith was unwavering. For the Christmas holidays Mami would take us to midnight mass on Christmas Eve and we loved it and she also allowed us to go caroling with the church through the neighborhood.

After I left for college, I continued in my Catholic faith, as I attended the only Black Catholic University — Xavier. In fact, my first Good Friday in New Orleans was a shocker. I remember leaving the dorm and heading over to Tia Lois' home for the weekend. That particular day, Tia Lois asked me if I wanted to go to the mall and I was appalled at the fact that mall was opened on Good Friday. She then explained to me that it was just another day in the United States and not a solemn day like in Panama. It took some getting used to for many years. While at Xavier University, I had the honor of meeting Pope John Paul II. I remember that day like it was yesterday. I was selected to be one of the few students to be in his presence while on our campus. The campus was on lock down for security reasons. I got dressed up and walked across a very lonely campus to get to the event. I was so elated to meet him and to have him put his hands on my forehead to bless me. When I got back to my room, I called Mami in Panama immediately and told her about my experience. Of, course she called everyone in the family to tell them about it. Mami was so proud of me. Over the years, I explored different religions and I shared with Mami what I was doing. She never tried to change my mind. She was just happy that I was worshipping and believed in God. She did not care what methodology I chose to worship and praise Him, as long as I did. After I moved to Georgia, I settled on a Christian church, Ray of Hope pastored by Cynthia L. Hale. A dynamic female pastor that served as an advisor for President Obama during his eight years at the White House. I love my pastor and so did my Mami when she came to visit. She would attend church with me. She enjoyed our choir and all the interactive praise and worship. She did not care that it was not Catholic. She just wanted to praise God and wanted me to do the same. I would introduce my Mami to my pastor every time she came in town and attended church with me. Mami did say to me once that she believed that women should be allowed to be priest, but she knew that the Catholic Church was never going to approve that.

Mami's faith was unwavering. Her faith kept us going many times. She would push us to believe when we were down and she prayed for all of us daily. She said her rosary and Catena prayer faithfully every day at 3 PM, which is the hour of the Divine Mercy. The time in which Christ died on the cross and the skies got dark and thunderous. Her television was fixed on the EWTN network, a global Catholic Television, Catholic Radio, and Catholic News Network that provides Catholic programming and news coverage from around the world. This is how she kept up to date with the whereabouts of the Pope and the changes in her Catholic faith. She watched the mass every day and on Sundays when she did not make it to St. Andrews. Mami kept a "Prayer List" with names of people that she prayed for daily. Many of my friends made that list and they don't even know it. Mami believed in her list and when I asked her to pray for any of my friends, she would request their full name and write it down. I had a dear friend Karen who died of cancer of August 13th, 2015, a day after my birthday. When Karen got sick five years prior, I asked Mami to pray for her and she put her on the list. I had a fundraiser for Karen at my home two years into her treatment when the medical bills were mounting. Mami and my nephews were in town for the summer and helped with organizing and arranging the basement. Mami had never met Karen until that day. But, they instantly connected when Mami shared that she was a cancer survivor and encouraged her to fight and fight hard like she did. Karen and Mami exchanged numbers and spoke often thereafter until her passing. I was so happy to share my Mother with Karen because I knew that she would make her feel better. Mami loved Karen and prayed for her until the end. Just another example of how her faith allowed her to connect with someone else and made their life better.

When my eldest sister Francie moved to the United States in 2012, she came to Georgia to live with me. Mami was already established in Indianapolis. One of the first things she wanted to make sure Francie did was to find a church home. Francie visited several churches including my own. But, she really wanted to reconnect with her strong Catholic faith. She settled on Christ Our Hope in Lithonia, Georgia. Francie has become a very active member of this church, in particular with Hispanic community. Attending mass in Spanish and directing the children's choir in Spanish also. When Mami would come to visit she would go to church with Francie. She still went with me occasionally, I guess she did not want me to feel left out. But, I understood that her faith was Catholic and her preference was to follow it. Francie also began making rosaries as a hobby. She gave most of them away. I have one hanging in my car. She made them as gifts and made several for Mami. Francie made a very special one for Mami that she placed in her hands the day of the funeral. When we decided to have Mami's services in Georgia, there was no doubt as to where the mass would be held and it was a beautiful home going service. Father JohnPaul had met Mami on several occasions and knew her enough to speak of her. His words were so fitting for her and comforted us so much. His message was right on point and he made it a celebration of life and not a mourning of death.

As her grandsons got older, she also instilled in them the notion of believing in a higher being. She ensured they went to church and as they got of age, they began to serve at St. Andrews. The pride in Mami's face when her grandkids would serve at Sunday mass said it all. Her pride overflowed via her smile, as they walked down the aisle. She saw both of them do their first communion at St. Andrews and that also filled her with joy. She gave them the daily blessings with one word, "bendiciones", which means blessings. Mami would not let anyone leave the house without that blessing. Even my brother-in-law would come see her prior to leaving to get his blessings. In fact, I could not hang up the phone without the last word being said by Mami….."bendiciones". I got so used to it, that I say it to my sister as she leaves the house for whatever reason and she says it to me too. These are the things that Mami taught us and we are passing down to the next generation because our faith has been deeply impacted and formed because of Mami's faith. Mami raised us to be individuals. We each have our own church homes and she encouraged and accepted that. For that, we thank her daily.

May 4th, 2017 was National Day of Prayer for 2017. I received an invitation from my colleague Dora to participate in the lunch time bible study and I accepted. A week prior Dora had invited me, but I was not able to attend. Also that same week, Dora called at around 8 PM on Tuesday. I was driving home after spending the evening with two dear friends at a "Spring Salads Demonstration" at Whole Foods in Alpharetta. I got in my car and memories of Mami began to overwhelm me. I was about to burst out in tears when the phone rang and it was Dora. She called to express her sympathy and to let me know that she had been praying for me. I told her that she was God sent at that moment. Because driving was one of the most difficult times of day. I would always call Mami while in my car and we would chat until I got home. Dora stayed on the phone with me until I pulled into my garage and I thanked her. Dora and I worked in Lima, Peru together in 2014. We attended a beautiful church one day for mass and we really enjoyed it. I have always known that Dora's faith was very strong and I admired her for it. She was not afraid to express her beliefs. Dora was my angel that day and I know that Mami sent her to me. *#Faith*

Foto Magia Photography

"*Quien no vive para servir, no sirve para vivir.*"

—Papa Francisco

Caring for the Elders

WHO IS A caretaker? One that gives emotional and physical care and support according to the definition of the word. Upon need, Mami was the one that the elders in the family turned to for care. Therefore, she was their "*caretaker*". Mami cared for her maternal aunt Lillian, who had asthma and was a very good seamstress. She then cared for her paternal uncle Carlos, who came to the house every day after selling his newspapers until he got older and she had to put him in a nursing home. Because she was caring for her own mother, Abuela. Although, culturally we do not believe in nursing homes in Panama, we do have them and it is the last choice. In the case of Tio Carlos, Mami had to do it and it was not the most pleasant experience for her. Mami also cared for her own parents and my Papi until they died. She was the caretaker in the family.

Tia Lillian lived close by our home and we would go visit her often after church because her apartment was in route. As Tia Lillian got older, her asthma seemed to get worse and Mami had to rush her to the hospital on several occasions. My most vivid memory of Tia Lillian was how great of a seamstress she was and how she would share sewing tips with Mami. Tia Lillian worked at a well-known department store named "Felix B. Maduro" in Panama until she retired. It was the equivalent of a "Macy's" or "Dillard's" in the United States. She did the alterations for customers who purchased clothing from the store. On the side, she also made clothing for people. We loved to visit Tia Lillian. She was my grandmother's youngest sister. Unfortunately, Tia Lillian's asthma became so bad that is took her life and Mami and my big sister Francie handled all the arrangements for her funeral. Mami had her remains placed in a mausoleum and would ensure that all payments were made on time. When Mami left Panama, she entrusted one of her besties, Yiniva, to continue making the payments for Tia Lillian. This is something that I need to follow up on now that Mami is gone.

Tio Carlos was her father's brother. I was told he was very popular with the ladies and in his younger days did very well for himself. He had an estranged son, which I never met. But, Mami knew him. Tio Carlos had his own little apartment downtown and did not want to move in with us. So he went back and forth daily. Sometimes, Papi or I would take him home if it was dark or raining. He was very independent. He was also a functional alcoholic. We used to watch him take his sips from his little small bottles of rum, which he purchased from the corner bodega. At times, we would hide his bottles from him and watch him look around for them. As children, we thought that was so funny. Not knowing the consequences of withdrawal. Tio Carlos grew older and could no longer care for himself and Mami placed him in a nursing home that was in operation by a group of nuns. Mami paid the monthly fee to have him there and she went to visit often. But, to my recollection she skipped a month or more due to other commitments and when she went to see him they told her he had died and that they did not know that he had family. Mami was so upset, I think she cursed at the nuns. Because they knew Mami came every month to pay his fees and she was his next of kin on the documentation she signed to register him. She was so upset and rightfully so. She cried and was sad for some time because she had no idea where his remains were placed. All she knew was that he was cremated and his remains were disposed of. It hurt my heart to hear her tell the story.

My GrandDaddy had a stroke and a heart attack when I was a child. He lived with us and I recall this part of my life clearly because he was in a coma for over a month. He suddenly woke up, but had lost his speech. Mami always said the he probably went too far while in the coma and God was not ready for him. Therefore, did not allow him to tell what he saw. GrandDaddy, as we called him lived for many years thereafter. He and Abuela traveled together several times to the United States on vacations. Between Abuela and Mami, they cared for him and ensured his wellbeing until the end. He lived a very good life regardless of his condition. We enjoyed him. He was playful and loved to imitate others. I was in middle school when my GrandDaddy died. It was my first experience with a funeral. I remember all the people that came to the house afterwards for the repast. It was not sad, because we were expecting it at the time. But it was still her father and she was sad to see him go. Daddy spoiled Mami as a child. He bought her everything. This is the one thing she would always tell us.

Next on the list was my Papi. He was stricken with cancer and battled for five years with Mami at his side. When he was first diagnosed, I was already living in New Jersey and working. I was twenty five years old and just getting my career as an engineer started. He was so proud of me. He referred to me as his daughter "the engineer" to his colleagues. They told me this at his funeral and it made me so proud in the midst of my sadness. Mami went with Papi back and forth to chemotherapy. He had several surgeries to remove parts of his colon. He had to wear a colostomy bag and Mami would clean his wound and replace the bag for him without thinking twice. He went into remission for a few years and then the cancer returned and metastasized. Papi then had a slight heart attack and his treatment had to be stopped. For many years, Mami was convinced that the gap in treatment is what caused his death. She believed that treatment was going to cure him just because she wanted to believe. In December of 1996, Papi transitioned peacefully. But, Mami had a hard time dealing with his death. He was the only man she had ever been with and married. He was the father of her three girls. I recall having to take time off my job to spend with Mami because she was not coping very well. Eventually, she bounced back and focused on living and taking care of Abuela. This is when they became travel partners.

Abuela was the last elder that Mami took care of. Mami loved her mother and was determined to give her the best care possible and that only meant doing it herself. Abuela loved living and being cared for by Mami. Abuela lost her sight due to glaucoma, but it did not stop her from living the rest of her life in a peaceful and grateful manner. Everyone loved Abuela, people would come to visit and just want to chat with her. She was well aware of her surroundings and although she could not see, she participated in conversations like she could. Mami called Abuela, the "computer" because her memory was so good. She did not forget any birthdays or anniversaries. She also did not forget names. Her mind was very sharp until the end. She was also very good with numbers. Abuela and Mami began traveling together to visit me in New Jersey. Then when my nephews were born, they spent most of their time in Indiana with them. While in Panama, Mami would take her to regular doctor visits and to visit friends and family. Early 2008, Abuela started saying she was not feeling well and started having these fainting spells. After evaluation by the doctors, we were told that she had pancreatic cancer. Once again, Mami had to deal with this horrible disease that she herself had beaten many years prior. We decided to come visit for Spring Break and we arrived in time because a few days later Abuela passed away and we were able to all be with her in last days and with Mami through the final process. Abuela was ninety six. She had lived a full, fun and adventurous life. We were proud of Mami for taking such good care of her for so long. I am convinced that Mami's care was the key to her long life. Abuela's funeral was a true celebration of life. I remember us dancing and singing all night after our guests left the house for the repast. Our neighbors could hear us and complimented the way we celebrated her life. We had a great time that night and it was exactly the way Abuela would have wanted us to remember her.

The year after Abuela died, Tio Joe, Mami's eldest brother began calling her very often and showing some signs of dementia. Mami would call me and express her concern about him. He lived in Brooklyn by himself. Tio Joe worked at a flower shop and delivered flowers by foot. He was well known in his community. He delivered flowers almost every day to the Twin Towers before the September 11th attacks. In fact, he did not have a delivery that day, which was odd. We were all worried about him when this event occurred because we knew that was a frequent building delivery for him. When we finally heard from him, we were all relieved that he was safe. The more Mami would call me to tell me that Tio Joe did not sound good, the more I knew I needed to follow in Mami's footsteps to care for the elderly in my family. So I went to Brooklyn, packed him up and moved him in with me in Stone Mountain, Georgia. It was an adjustment for him because he was a "city guy". I live in the suburbs and you need a car to get anywhere. I remember when I picked him up from his apartment and we crossed the Verrazano bridge and I heard him whisper, "now my loneliness ends" in Spanish. That was confirmation that I had done the right thing. For the next couple of weeks, I struggled to get him situated and adjusted to his new life style. Unfortunately, Tio Joe was only with me for six months. I am convinced that he knew he was ill and was not going to last long and wanted to be around family. That summer of 2009, he was able to see all of his siblings, nieces and nephews before he died. I cared for Tio Joe, just like Mami cared for Tia Lillian and Tio Carlos, whom did not have any kids. I did what I learned from watching Mami and I did it well. I have no regrets because I know that in Tio Joe's last days he was surrounded by his family.

I think I know why God took the "Caretaker" when he did. Mami had cared for Daddy, Tia Lillian, Tio Carlos, Papi and Abuela in that order. Mami was a faithful servant of God. Each of those family members had a lot of suffering in their final days. Mami paid her dues in advance when she cared for them and God was not going to allow her to suffer or deteriorate. So he snatched her just in time to avoid that. He took her because her work was done and well done. This notion gives me comfort every time I think of it. It has helped me to accept the loss of Mami. I shared it with my baby sister Maritza and her response was, "if I think of it like that, it makes it easier to see". I will continue to look at it in this manner because it is healing and it also speaks to the power of God and His decisions. *#Caretaker*

Being a Godmother

WHAT IS A Godparent? A Godparent, in many denominations of Christianity, is someone who sponsors a child's baptism. Today, the word Godparent does not always have explicitly religious overtones. The secular view of a Godparent tends to be an individual chosen by the parents to take an interest in the child's upbringing and personal development, and to take care of the child should anything happen to the parents.

Being a Godmother was the other role that Mami took on very seriously, besides motherhood. Her godchildren were "Her" children also! Mami is my best example of being a Godmother. She has seven godchildren (Tony, Xiomara, Gisela, Tyra, Karen, Freddie and Edwin) and we knew all of them very well. They spent summers and holidays with us. It was so hard to notify them when she passed. They were all so hurt with her passing and have supported my sisters and me through this process. They, like us, miss having that confidant to chat with and get advice from.

Mrs. Amy was Mami's Godmother. We grew up hearing this name all the time. Mami had a close relationship with her. I remember her taking us to her apartment in Panama to visit her and I recall her having birds in cages and we would sit and watch them while she and Mami would catch up. She then moved to San Juan, Puerto Rico where she lived the rest of her life. But, Mami kept in touch with her until she passed. She always spoke so highly of her Godmother. She had such fond memories of my Abuela taking her to visit Mrs. Amy and shared those with us. I also recall her sending her Christmas cards and asking us to drop them in the mail upon our return to the United States. Since we would come home to Panama for the holidays and it was more secure and reliable to mail from the United States to Puerto Rico. At some point, the Christmas cards were returned and no answer. Upon investigation we found out the Mrs. Amy had passed away. I was hurt for my Mami because I knew how close they were. But I cherished the fact that I experienced Mrs. Amy with and through Mami.

Mami's eldest godson, Tony adored his Godmother or "Madrina", the Spanish translation. He still speaks so highly of her. Mami was a dear friend of his mother, Mrs. Julie until she died. It was amazing to see how close Mami and Tony were and how they would converse on the phone all the time. I was always curious about the nature of the conversation. But I never asked. I only imagined that it was like my conversations with my Godmother Neva. Over the years, after Mami moved to Indianapolis, she continued to connect with Tony and have conversation with him. She supported him throughout his mother's illness and her death. I remember back in Panama when he would come back to visit from the United States and he was tall and handsome and it always struck me how childlike he would be around her. His respect and honor for her was admirable. He treasured her and his relationship with her. When Mami passed, we were actually in the Bahamas vacationing and as I went through in my head who we needed to notify, Tony was one of the first people that came to mind. We looked in Mami's luggage and realized she did not have her "little black book" of contacts. She had left it at home. So I asked my family members if they knew how to reach him and no one did. Therefore, I had to wait for us to return to the United States to get to that book and call him. My sister Maritza made the initial contact to let him know and he was so hurt to hear about her sudden death. My heart then told me that I need to need to reconnect with him myself and I asked Maritza for his number. I reached out to him via text message and he responded immediately. He asked for photographs of Mami's services and I sent to him via WhatsApp and we spent the day reconnecting. He sent photos of himself and his siblings. He said in case we crossed each other on the streets, we would recognize each other. Tony also shared his address with me and I sent him a copy of the program from the services. He was so grateful for me reaching out and sharing the photos with him. He was not able to attend the services because of a recent surgery. But, we knew that he was there in spirit. I promised Tony to visit him whenever I was in the Virginia area. In fact, I looked up his address and noticed he is close to another dear friend from high school. I had already promised her I would visit her this year. So the plan is to see Tony at the same time. All I could think was that this is very small world and the more we talk to people, the closer we seem to actually be. I totally believe in six degrees of separation.

Mami's goddaughter Xiomara I remember because of her grandmother, Mrs. Dora. We would visit them every time we went downtown and Mrs. Dora would have raisin bread and a coca cola for us to have every time we visited. She lived in an apartment building and Mami would take us to see the carnival parade with Xiomara because it was right on the parade route. Xiomara also lived in the same apartment building, but a few floors up. I also remember for Christmas and birthdays how Mami would pick a gift for Xiomara and ensure that it was something that she would like and would nail it every time. Over the years, we lost touch with Xiomara, but not Mami. She kept in touch with her and with her mother. I do vividly remember when Mrs. Dora died and how during her last years when she was stricken with Alzheimer's, the one person she never forgot was Mami. Mami would go visit her and she would always remember her, as "Jeannie". This is another testimony of the person Mami was. She was unforgettable and not even a disease as such could erase her from Dora's memory. I reconnected with Xio when I went to Panama in May, 2017. I called her mother to get her cell phone number and I gave her a call. We connected via WhatsApp and exchanged photos of each other. I sent her photos of Mami and told her that I was writing the book. It was so good to hear from her. We vowed to stay in touch and do better.

Gisela is my childhood friend. We grew up together in Panama playing in the streets and always laughing. When we decided to do our "Confirmation" together, she chose Mami to be her confirmation Godmother and I chose Mami's other dear friend Yiniva as my confirmation Godmother. Gisela and Mami quickly developed a great relationship. She called Mami "Madrina", which is the translation for Godmother in Spanish. That was the only name for her coming from Gisela's mouth. Mami stood by Gisela through many difficult times and Gisela confided in her on many things. I must say that at times, I felt some a twinge of jealousy due to their closeness. But, I quickly got over it because I knew that is just who Mami was. When Mami passed, there was no doubt that Gisela would be present for her services in Stone Mountain, Georgia. Mami even forged a strong bond with Gisela's mother. They became really good friends and supported each other. They were neighbors. These bonds warmed my heart when I would come back to Panama to visit because they allowed me to know that Mami was in good hands while I was not home or around. I had "people" I could call to check on her if I needed to.

My godsister Tyra, she is the daughter of Mami's dear friend, Tia Janet. Mami's bond with Tia Janet goes way back. Mami helped raise her first child, whom they called "Chiquitin" back then. In fact, before Mami married Papi, many people rumored that Papi was marrying some girl with a child, not knowing she was doing a friend a favor. Unfortunately, Chiquitin and Mami lost touch after he grew up and left Panama. Mami accepted to be Tyra's Godmother and she served her so well. Tyra would come to visit us in Panama for the summer and stay for months. She was an inner city Philly child. Therefore, she was not used to bugs. I was and loved them. I chased Tyra once with a dragonfly and she screamed in one breath all around the yard until Mami came out and told me I was going to give that child a heart attack. I thought that was so funny. Tyra eventually got used to the outdoors and fit right in with the "The Little Rascals of Panama", as we called ourselves. As Tyra got older she found a confidant in Mami. Tyra would come to Mami about everything. I know this because Tyra would tell me about her conversations with Mami and let me know how beautiful her relationship with Mami was. Mami kept a tight lip with anything that Tyra told her. She also served as a liaison between her and her own mother every time they had a disagreement. Tyra was so comfortable with Mami and I encouraged her to continue sharing with Mami because I knew it was healthy to have someone to listen and advise you. I was always so willing to share Mami's gift with others and I did. Tyra is a nurse and she told me that it was because of Mami's encouragement to go back to school and get a degree that she finished the nursing program. She looked at her godsisters and saw what they were doing and wanted to follow in their footsteps. Mami's education influenced went beyond her biological children. I recall having to call Tyra to notify her of Mami's death and the scream that followed through the phone broke my heart. I knew she would take it really hard and I was so hurt for her. Mami was her "go to" person. I knew that a void had been created right at that second and I prayed for her for my days to come. I called her to see how she was doing in the midst of my loss. But I knew that was something that Mami would want me to do.

My cousin Freddie, who is also my god brother is a fraternal twin. He loved his Tia Jean and his Godmommy. At one point, I actually forgot he was her godson because I saw him as her nephew first. But, they didn't forget. It was front and center for both of them. They had a special bond because of the dual connection. He is the son of Mami's baby sister, Brenda. I have a similar bond with my nephew Jalen. He is also my godchild, so I know what that feels like. It is different and special. I recall Mami having such an affinity for Freddie. She would speak of him so tenderly and always looked out for him. This year, it was Mami that reminded me of Freddie's birthday. Although, her memory had been failing, when it came to birthdays of her godchildren, she never forgot. Her long term memory was impeccable until the end.

Karen is the daughter of one of Mami's best friends, Yiniva. Yiniva is my sister Francie's baptismal Godmother and my confirmation Godmother. We are all intertwined via God and long termed friendships. Yiniva and Mami became friends while being co-workers. Yiniva took care of Mami while she was pregnant with Francie. They became very good friends and remained this way until the end. When Karen was born, there was no doubt who Yiniva would want as her Godmother. Karen was a beautiful baby with long flowing hair and she looked like a doll. We quickly embraced her as our little sister. Karen would come and spend days at our home and we would play together all day long. We would also ensure nothing happened to her. She was the youngest of all of us. Over the years, Karen and her Madrina became closer regardless of the distance between them. Mami did not allow physical distance to interfere with her spiritual bond with her Godchildren. Mami kept up with Karen and Yiniva via telephone. A phone call with Yiniva meant hours on the phone. They chatted about everything. I remember how excited Mami was when Karen had her first child, Sofia. She was born the same year as Mami's second grandson, Jalen. It was a special year for Mami. Two new babies in the family. Karen and Yiniva are considered family and no one could tell her or us otherwise.

Edwin aka "Pocho" is the baby of all her godchildren and we knew it. Because she treated him as such. Pocho would come and spend time with us during the summer. We loved to tease him about his sweaty hands. We also played with his hair because it was straight like an Asian and would stand up on the top of his head. We thought that was funny and he did too. I recall vividly his ritual prior to getting in bed at night. He loved to walk bare feet all day long. So before bed, Mami would make us take a shower. He would sit on the edge of the bed and rub his feet together to get all the dust off prior to getting in bed. We thought that was so funny. As you can see, we had many laughs with Pocho growing up. Mami had a special place in her heart for Pocho. She supported him in times of need and he felt comfortable reaching out to her at any time. The pain that Pocho expressed with the death of his Madrina was painful to see. But this is just confirmation of the strong bonds Mami had created with all of her godchildren.

I have the best Godmother, Neva. She was Mami's BFF (Best Friend Forever). They had been friends since Mami was seven years old. I always wondered why Neva was my Godmother and I was not the first born. Therefore, one day I asked Mami why. She responded that the Catholic church is very strict about Godparents being Catholic and Neva was not Catholic. The particular church where she wanted to baptize my big sister Francie only permitted for Catholic Godparents. Therefore, Mami asked her other bestie, Yiniva. By the time I came along, the church that Mami chose to baptize me in did not have that strict requirement and Neva was able to be my Godmother. I feel blessed to be the lucky one to have gotten

Neva, Mami's best friend forever. Neva and I have been close from day one. Over the years, as I became an adult, I cherished our relationship even more than ever. She has served her role as "Godmother" extremely well. Before my Godmother returned to Panama after Mami's funeral, she looked at me and said, "I am your Mother now", and that warmed my heart. She has always been there for me and continues to be because that is how Mami would want it. I also have a second Godmother, Yiniva. She is my confirmation Godmother. In the Catholic religion you get to have two Godmothers officially and I chose Mami's other best friend because I knew it was the perfect combination for me. I call Yiniva "Madrina". Madrina has always been there for me. She has also traveled to come visit Mami and stay in my home in Georgia. I always knew when Mami was on the phone with Madrina because she would be on the phone for hours. They loved to chat and laugh together and I loved it.

I have eight godchildren (Malcolm, Jalen, Brycen, Brayden, Madison, Samantha, Emily and Gabriel). I don't have any biological children of my own. I finally beat Mami, so sorry she did not live long enough to see me beat her family record. Up until Mami's death I had six godchildren total. But, I asked my dear friend/soror Maritza Garcia Williams, if I could be the Godmother to her two precious daughters (Samantha and Madison). At the time, they considered me an "Auntie". But for some reason my heart kept telling me that I needed to be more than that to them. So for the first time, I asked to take the responsibility and their parents accepted it with open arms. I think every child should have a godparent. Someone outside of their parents that they can go to. I take being a "G-Mama" very seriously. I get it from Mami. Some of my godchildren's siblings think I am their Godmother too. Simply because, I also treat them with love and have a relationship with them. If you are a godparent, ensure that you are connected to that child and fulfill the promise that you made to their parents and to God when you accepted the responsibility. I would also suggest that when you have children close in age, consider having the same godparents for them, if possible. This way if something happens to you and the godparents have to take over, as they should, the children won't be separated. If not possible, ensure that all of your children's godparents know each other because they should all have to collectively take over if something happens to the parents. These are just suggestions based on my own life experiences.

So, if you have a godchild or godparent you have not spoken to in a while, reach out to them. It is your responsibility. You made a promise to God to do so and you should. The main reason I could write this chapter with such meticulous details about each of her godchildren is because she was the perfect "Madrina". She ensured that her godchildren were like her children and she exposed us all to them like siblings. Mami is a great example of being a "Godmother" and I am proud to say that I learned from the best and I have earned my "G-Mama" stripes. I plan to continue to put into practice the lessons that Mami taught me about being a Godmother. I promise to be a part of their lives as long as I have breath in my body, as Mami did with her godchildren. *#G-Mami*

Sisterhood beyond Bloodlines

A SISTERHOOD IS NOT necessarily formed by people who are blood related. A sisterhood is something that is forged, developed, nurtured and kept regardless of whom you were born from. My Mami understood this so perfectly, that she became my example of how I should form my friendships/sisterhood to sustain me through life changing events. Mami had two bloodline sisters. But, because of the 10 and 13 year gap in age, she was forced to establish a sisterhood with her friends prior to the arrival of her siblings. The following is a description of Mami's sisterhood with women who have been a part of our lives and made such a difference in hers also.

Neva Hunt-Edwards:

The first sisterhood that she formed was with my Godmother Neva. They met living on Galvez building in Panama City, Panama when Mami was just seven years old. Their connection was instant and it lasted a lifetime. Neva was without any doubt her Best Friend Forever (BFF). As children, they played together all day long. Neva told me that my GrandDaddy would buy Mami whatever she wanted. She said he just spoiled her. But, she benefitted from it because Mami would share whatever he bought her with Neva. Neva said Mami had a briefcase filled with paper dolls and that they would play all day long with them switching their outfits and dressing them up. They would also play jacks for hours and Mami was a pro at this game. They played with as many as one hundred jacks. My GrandDaddy also bought Mami a kitchen set. It was made of stainless steel and I remember it, because it was so well made that she was able to pass down the stove to us and we enjoyed playing with it and having it restored with a can of spray paint whenever it started to get rusty.

Neva and Mami became inseparable. According to Mami people would call them "Salt & Pepper" and "Mutt & Jeff". They did everything together. Through photographs, I would experience those good times that they had double dating with whom will become their respective husbands. Although, both Mami and Neva had siblings of their own, the bond they had forged as children did not allow for that sisterhood to be broken by anyone. Their friendship was admirable and envied by others. It is very hard to find friends with such a history these days. Neva prided herself in always telling me that she and Mami never had a fight. Not to say they agreed on everything. But they respectfully disagreed. Neva has very fond memories of my grandparents growing up on Galvez building. They were neighbors and she recalls my GrandDaddy, aka "Mr. Alleyne", walking every morning to the bathroom to take his shower singing: "Oh what a beautiful morning, oh what a beautiful day". The same way "Mami" was a household name for us, so was "Neva" or "Ms. Neva". We heard that name from the day we were born. I remember going on short trips to the zoo and Canal Zone with Neva always being there with us. When Neva had her one and only son, he became our god brother because Papi was his Godfather. So that bond was extended to another generation through the godparentships. I remember Leo spending a lot of time at our home playing with us. We had a big home and our doors were always open. He loved spending the night and Neva had no worries because she knew "Jeannie" was going to care for him, as if he was hers and she did.

Yiniva Córdoba:

They met working as young ladies. They were both single, but Mami was engaged to Papi when they met. They were co-workers at the "Europea" furniture store. Mami worked in the accounting department and Yiniva was the assistant to the General Manager's secretary. Yiniva and Mami became very close and she would help Mami during her first pregnancy. She was there by her side the entire time. When I called Yiniva to tell her that I had decided to write a book about Mami, she shared that she had started writing about Mami also. She wrote a letter in memory of Mami. The letter speaks for itself. It describes the depth of their friendship and how much she misses her dear friend. I asked if I could include her letter in this book and she agreed. Therefore, I have translated it below and also included the Spanish version in her own handwriting, thereafter:

"In Memoriam of My Friend, Jean Ford

Your sudden departure to the Celestial Homeland took me by surprise. It saddened me and it will take time for me to assimilate it all at once.

You were my soul sister, my friend, my confidant, almost a spiritual director and counselor. When we both met, we were both single women. I remember clearly, your small waist and bumble bee butt, and your feet were so small, a size three, that you had to go to a shoemaker to have them custom made to your size and style.

You adopted me, as little sister, (I was seven years younger than you). You used to tell me that I was too goofy. In other words, a young and naïve girl. I thank you for all the wonderful times we spent together, for allowing me to be a part of your family and to have helped in carrying the burdens during difficult times.

You were an attentive listener, a counselor filled with wisdom. We shared in each other's happy and sad moments. When they diagnosed you with the uterine cancer, certainly Neva was able to be by your side more than I could. You were an exemplary mother, wife, daughter and loving sister. You never thought twice in leaving your job to solely engage in the wellbeing of your daughters, husband and your parents.

During our last conversation on the phone, of almost an hour (fifteen days before your final departure), you seemed a bit nostalgic, maybe a presage of what was to come. I do not remember why we discussed your arts and crafts and I told you that I still had the ceramic doll dressed up in a "ballroom dress".

I felt a smile come about on your face. You really enjoyed knowing that I still had her. You even told me that you wondered what might have happened to that doll. That was your favorite work of art. I even told you that I had her on my night table and that way you were always present with me.

I was present with you during your pregnancy with Francella. We would go home together after work. You lived in an apartment located on Via Porras. I would stay with you until Oscar (R.I.P.) came home with his great big smile and a pint of ice cream! That was the reason why Francie weighed ten pounds. She was a beautiful ebony baby. Afterwards, Angie was born, who looked a lot like Oscar (R.I.P.). Lastly, Maritza was born whom you wished were a boy, but by surprised another girl. I went with you to receive your first grandchild, AJ.

You were Karen's Godmother, my only child. You and Oscar would take her during the summer vacations and you treated her like another daughter. That is how your home was, a safe haven, a place of peace and love. The kids on the block loved to come to the garage, Oscar said you were "the old lady in the shoe house", because your house was always full of kids and you would take care of them all, with your usual sympathy.

Good-bye my beloved friend, the memories will continue to flow little by little, I have so many to remember of our more than fifty years of friendship. We knew to respect our private lives. We never argued. We had very little disagreements, but you had the maturity to forgive and forget.

I know that you are in God's mansion, that Jesus, Divine Mercy, tells you: "Come blessed one of my Father", rest in peace, beloved friend."

En Memoria.
Mi amiga. Jean Ford

Tu partida a la Patria Celestial me tomó de sorpresa. Me entristeció y tomará tiempo que lo asimila. Fuistes mi hermana del alma, mi amiga, mi confidente, casi mi directora espiritual y consejera. Nos conocimos las dos solteras. Te recuerdo claramente: Tu figura de muñeca bien formada con tu "nalga de avispa". Tus pies pequeños talla 3 por lo que tenías que ir a un zapatero para encargarlos hechos a tu medida y modelo seleccionado. Me adoptastes como a una hermana menor (yo soy siete años menor que tú). Me decías que yo era una "bobita". En otras palabras, una poca ingenua. Gracias por todos esos gratos momentos compartidos. Por hacerme parte de tu familia y sobrellevarme en mis momentos difíciles. Fuistes un oído atento, una consejera llena de sabiduría. Vivimos juntas los momentos alegres y tristes de cada una. Cuando te diagnos

trataron el cancer uterino. Aunque
Nueva te podía acompañar más del que
fuistes madre ejemplar, esposa, hija,
hermana amorosa. No dudaste
en dejar de trabajar para sólo dedicarte
al bienestar de tus hijas, esposo
y tus padres.

Durante nuestra última charla
telefónica de casi una hora (15 días
antes de tu partida final) te sentí
nostálgica; quizás presintiendo...
No recuerdo porque hablamos de tus
manualidades y te comenté que
yo tenía la muñeca de cerámica
vestida con "ballroom dress".
Se sintió sonreír. Te gustó saber
que yo la tenía. Me dijistes "me
preguntaba qué habría sido de ella"
Era una de tus obras favoritas. Te
comenté que la tenía engalanando
mi mesita de noche. Así que
siempre te tenía presente.

Te acompañé en tu primer embarazo,
Francella. Nos íbamos juntas a la
salida del trabajo. Uds. vivían en un
apartamento ubicado Vía Parras. Yo me
quedaba contigo hasta que llegaba
Óscar (qepd) con su gran sonrisa
y una pinta de helado!

Por eso Joanne pesó 10 lbs. Era una hermosa bebé de ébano. Luego nació Angie tan parecida a Oscar (q.e.p.d.) Por último Maritza que deseaban fuese varón pero resultó otra niña. Te acompañé a recibir tu primer nieto, A.J.

Tú fuiste la madrina de Karen, mi única hija. Tú y Oscar la recibían en verano, para las vacaciones y la tratabas como una hija más.

Así era tu hogar: Un remanso de paz y amor. La chiquillada de la calle le gustaba llegar al garaje de tu casa. Oscar decía que tú eras: "The old lady in the blue house". Porque tu casa siempre estaba llena de niños y tú los atendías con tu usual simpatía.

Adiós, querida amiga, los recuerdos seguirán fluyendo poco a poco. Tengo tanto que recordar de nuestros más de 50 años de amistad.

Supimos respetar nuestra vida privada. Nunca discutimos. Pocas veces tuvimos desacuerdos pero tú tenías la madurez para perdonar y olvidar.

Sé que estás en la Casa del Padre. Que Jesús, Divina Misericordia.

Yiniva is my eldest sister Francie's baptism Godmother and she is my confirmation Godmother. We both call her "Madrina". I had a great visit with Yiniva when I returned to Panama in May, 2017. We sat down and she handed me the original letter and we just reminisced about Mami.

Elena Cole:

These two became friends through their husbands. Tia Elena's husband, Stafford, frequented the Army/Navy store where Mami and Papi worked together. Papi managed the store and Mami was Mr. Berger's secretary. Mr. Berger was the owner. So Tio Cole, as we called him, would go purchase pants for his father and he and Papi became friends. Soon thereafter, Mr. Berger opened a new distribution store called Superior Products (Supro), Mami and Papi moved over to that store to work for him. Also Tio Cole followed and became their accountant and this is how the friendship began. Mami and Tia Elena became very close friends because they began to socialize together. The Coles would always have a Christmas party and they would always come over for Mami's 3rd of November birthday celebration. Tia Elena had three sons, one of which passed away in a car accident many years ago. Mami was there for her to support her through her grief. I recall exactly where I was when I got the news that my cousin had died. Both families are so close that everyone continues to believe that we are blood related. I could always tell when Mami was on the phone with Tia Elena because there was always a lot of laughter or gossiping. Those two were like two peas in a pod. After Mami left Panama, she kept in touch with Tia Elena via telephone and email. Tia Elena has a Magic Jack, so they could chat anytime at a very low cost and they did. Tia Elena told me that a few days before Mami left for the Bahamas trip that they spoke on the phone for a very long time. They even laughed at how long they had been on the phone not knowing that would be the last conversation they would ever have. Tia Elena misses her weekly conversations with Mami and continues to call and check on us to ensure that we are coping well with the loss. I went back to Panama to visit family in May, 2017. My first stop was the Coles home. I sat with both my aunt and uncle and we talked about Mami and I told them all about the services. These two people are permanent fixtures in my life and there is no way that I could come to Panama without seeing them. My memories of our time with Coles is filled with laughter, dancing, food and nothing but fun. We plan to come back to Panama in December, 2017 for Christmas and New Year. The Coles have already extended the invitation for us to join them on Christmas day for old time sake.

Janet Holland:

Mami helped raise Tia Jan's first child, whom they called "Chiquitin". This child went everywhere with Mami. To the point where people though it was her child. In fact, Papi's eldest sister once said that he was marrying a woman that had a child not knowing that she was just helping a friend. Tia Jan as we call her, was Mami's classmate and would come over after school and spend most of her time at Mami's house. Abuela and my great grandmother would make her something to eat. This was all when they lived on the Canal Zone. Tia Jan says that Abuela always treated her like another one of her daughters and that she would lay in the bed and have long conversations with her. Tia Jan would spend time in the backyard picking fruits from the trees with Abuela. When Mami married Papi, Chiquitin was the ring bearer at their wedding. They always told the story that after he walked the ring down the aisle on the pillows and delivered them, he then asked "what do I do with this, throw it away?" He was referring to the pillow and they all laughed. For many years, they would remember this and laugh all over again. Tia Jan, left Panama and moved to the United States in 1957. But, would come back often on vacation. She came back right when Francie was born. Tia Jan and Mami celebrated many 3rd of Novembers together. They would go watch the parade and see Tia Jan's sister Maria play the drums.

Mami would call Tia Jan at least once a week. When Mami would call Tia Jan, the first thing she would say is "hey Mrs. Janet". Tia Jan misses those phone calls because Mami would keep her up to date with the kids and what each of us were doing. Tia Jan says that she reached for the phone recently to call "Jeannie", as she called her and was sadden when she realized that was not possible. Jeannie was her best friend and had been by her side through thick and thin. Mami was her only daughter's Godmother. Tia Jan misses Mami so much and thinks about her every night before she goes to bed.

Dorothea Goldson:

She is Papi's sister and was more than a sister-in-law to Mami. She was Mami's friend and hairdresser. They met when Papi and Mami worked at the Army & Navy store in Panama. Tia Dorothea had a hair salon and did Mami's hair for many years. She would always fuss at Mami for wanting a perm in her hair because she already had naturally soft and silky hair. Tia Dorothea and Mami spent a lot of time together partying and just having a good time because Tia Dorothea loved to throw parties. Tia Dorothea refers to Mami as just a "beautiful person" and the best sister-in-law you could ever ask for. Tia Dorothea thinks about Mami all the time and she catches herself when she goes to pick up the phone to call her and then the sadness sets in once again because she can't talk to her. Their frequent phone calls is what she misses the most about Mami. Now that Mami is gone, I am finding out how many people Mami would call and chat with and how they all miss those phone calls. I remember growing up in Panama and meeting Tia Dorothea. She had moved from Panama to the United States but would always come back to visit. She is always so loving and soft spoken with us. I recall in particular that she loved gold jewelry and she would have a lot of it. She was the first person that I ever met with a nose ring and I thought that was so cool. She was unique and was very fond of Mami. You could see the warmth in their relationship. It is making me smile as a write about it. It was evident that they considered each other sisters. A few years ago Tia Dorothea decided to move to Georgia from Delaware. This would put her closer to family. When Mami would come to visit me in Georgia, I would always make sure that they saw each other. I would either go get Tia Dorothea and bring her back to my home to spend the weekend or I would take Mami to her home to visit. No way would Mami come to Georgia without seeing her. In 2016 when Mami was in Georgia visiting me, we decided to go have lunch at Olive Garden and we picked up Tia Dorothea and headed to the restaurant. As we waited to be seated, Mami and Tia Dorothea just engaged in conversation and I just watched them. My big sister Francie was also with us. We enjoyed our lunch and then we dropped her off at home. I believe that was the last time Mami and Tia Dorothea spent time together. Tia Dorothea misses her phone calls with Mami. If there was a phone line to heaven, I think Mami's phone would be ringing off the hook.

Sra. Melva Worrell Osakwe:

Mrs. Melva, as she preferred for us to call her. Mrs. Melva is very formal and did not want us to address her by her first name. Therefore, we respect that. She was a lot stricter with her kids than Mami was with hers. She met Mami when they were young adolescents. They became very close friends and she also spent a lot of time at Mami's house, where Abuela would cook for them and allow them to just enjoy themselves. Mrs. Melva knew Mami before she met Papi. They double dated together while Mami lived on the Canal Zone. At the age of nineteen, Mrs. Melva left for the United States to study nursing. She worked to pay her tuition. Before leaving, Mami bought her a bunch of underwear to take on her trip. She is still grateful for this. She and Mami kept in touch regardless of the distance. Mrs. Melva then moved to Africa where she lived for many years. She would send correspondence and post cards to Mami. Mami would share those with us and we were so excited to know someone that lived in Africa. Mami often spoke of her friend that lived in Africa. It sounded so exotic and Mami was very proud to say it. Over the years, they remained friends via phone calls and letters. Mrs. Melva would always come visit Mami when she would return to Panama. I remember meeting her kids for the first time also. Mrs. Melva returned to the United States and lives in New York. When Mami moved to Indianapolis, she kept in touch with her via frequent phone calls. I asked Mrs. Melva what she could share with me about Mami. She told me that Mami was easy going and never created any trouble and that she got along with everyone. She said that Mami was good with the kids and was a very reliable friend. When my baby sister Maritza called Mrs. Melva to tell her about Mami's passing, she was instantly saddened. She began to make plans to attend the services and she did. She paid her final respects to Mami with her presence and we are forever grateful to her for that.

Jovita Ruiz:

Jovita and Mami were neighbors in La Boca on the Canal Zone and school classmates. Their fathers were very good friends. As young adults, they both would go to Sacred Heart Church in Balboa and pray to the Virgin of Fatima. Sacred Heart Church is where Jovita ended up getting married. Jovita has three sons: Yeyito, Fabian and Javier. Yeyito lived in the United States with her sister, who is a nurse. Tia Jovita, as we called her, was our personal travel agent. She made all of our travel reservations when I was a child and even when I was in college. I recall going to her office to pick up our paper tickets and she walking Mami through what everything meant on the tickets. She ensured that we never had any problems during our travels and she was always looking out for the best deals for Mami. Tia Jovita is five feet tall, just like Mami, they actually look like they could be related. They treated each other like sisters. In Panama there is a tradition that if you go visit a newborn, you should bring a gift just as the three wise men brought to Jesus. When I was born, Tia Jovita came to the hospital to see me without a gift. Therefore, she took her jade and gold pendant off and gave to Mami as a gift to me. I still have that pendant and it holds sentimental value for me. I was so moved by her actions when Mami told me about it. Tia Jovita lived in the Miami for several months and would travel back and forth to Panama. She had family there and she also worked part time while there. Her son Javier was so fond of Mami and they would chat on the phone all the time. Tia Jovita would also bring him to visit Mami at her home in Panama. Even after Mami moved to Indiana, she would still call to chat with Jovita and her son. It was heartwarming to see Mami talk to him. She treated him with such tender loving care and Jovita appreciated it so much. Growing up, I remember Tia Jovita being one of those people that would join in the 3rd of November birthday celebration for Mami. I also remember going with Mami on Christmas Eve to deliver gifts to her home for her and her family. My baby sister received a beautiful card from Tia Jovita addressed to her nieces and also signed by her son Javier to express their sympathy.

Beverly Rondon:

Beverly and Mami met at work. Beverly was hired as a temporary secretary to replace Mami while she was out on maternity leave with my baby sister Maritza. Beverly had just graduated from high school when she came to work at Supro. This was the beginning of a lifetime friendship. One that lasted over forty seven years, the same age as Maritza, at the time of Mami's death. When Mami returned from her leave, Beverly was prepared to be let go. But, instead they kept her and let go of the other secretary. Mami taught Beverly the ropes and she learned very quickly. Mami was a great writer in English and Spanish. She could also type very fast and she was very productive. Mami shared all her skills with Beverly to bring her up to speed. Beverly considered her to be an excellent professional. When my parents built their home in Rio Abajo a suburb in Panama City, they invited Beverly to the housewarming and this is how their friendship began to flourish outside of work. They would spend their lunch hour going to eat at Mrs. Jessie's home. Mrs. Jessie would cook gourmet lunches for the entire Supro crew. Mami and Beverly began hanging outside of work. Beverly was a party host and Mami's home became "Party Central". Mami would allow Beverly to have all her birthday parties at her home. They both had birthdays in November and Beverly celebrated the entire month. Beverly, Elena and Mami became a trio because of their work connections. Beverly says that Mami was her family. She was more than a friend. Mami was her sister. Beverly's mother adored Mami and Mami visited her often because they lived close by. Beverly would call Mami the "Great Jean Ford" and Mami would blush and laugh every time she said it. Mami was honored by the title Beverly had given her. Beverly decided to move to the United States, but they vowed to not let the distance separate them. They would write letters to each other and over the years with technology, they began to send emails. I got Mami a laptop and taught her how to use it. At first she was just using it to play games like solitaire. Then I created a Yahoo email account for her and showed her how to use it. Mami and Beverly would communicate daily via email. They really enjoyed that interaction. Mami would forward emails from Beverly daily and this is how I knew how often they communicated. Any jokes or prayers that she got from Beverly, she would forward on to us. For many years as a child, I did not understand the relationship between Mami and Beverly. All we knew was that she is our "Tia". She treats us like nieces and we loved it. When I had a chance to speak with Beverly about Mami, she told me how much she misses her chats with Mami because she learned so much from her. Beverly said that Mami was always so peaceful and that she loved to dance also. My memories of Beverly and Mami are so happy. I can still see them laughing in my mind because that is all they did.

P. Merle Wade:

I became a member of Delta Sigma Theta Sorority, Inc. back in 1994. I had always wanted to be a part of this sorority. Unfortunately, as a basketball player at Xavier University, I could not pledge into any of these organizations. But, I worked very closely with them and connected with many of the members of the Gamma Alpha Chapter. Therefore, I knew a lot about Delta. I then committed to pledging graduate chapter when I moved to New Jersey. I met a fellow engineer Michelle Byrd-Fielder while volunteering for a program named PACE in New Brunswick. The program consisted of exposing high school students to careers in engineering. I found out through Michelle that the Central Jersey Alumnae Chapter was going to have a line. She provided me with all the information to apply, I did and made it into the sorority. This is where I met P. Merle Wade, a soror that I connected with like a mother. Merle, as many knew her, had a daughter Karen, who was also a member of the chapter. Merle and I conversed many a times during sorority meeting and outside of the meeting. She lived five minutes from my home in New Jersey, so I visited her often. I loved to visit because her home was so warm and she had a nice porch with lots of plants and flowers. It reminded me of Mami's home in Panama. Merle reminded me of a "Southern Belle", her beauty, hospitality and kindness overflowed at all times and it was so easy to be around her, just like Mami. When my father passed in 1996, Merle sent me a beautiful card with a lovely note. She asked me for Mami's address in Panama and she sent Mami a letter. That was the beginning of a beautiful "Pen Pal" friendship. Mami was so grateful for her kind words and she reciprocated with a response letter. This went back and forth for many years and I loved it. Two women that meant so much to me had connected and never laid eyes on each other. Soon after my Papi's death, I moved to Georgia. When Mami would come to visit, she would make sure to call Merle and they would chat on the phone. I watched her joy during the conversation and when I would chat with Merle she would also share in the delight of having had a conversation with Mami. They became sisters and Mami loved the fact that I had another mother figure that was physically closer to me. She cherished that and she loved Merle for it. Mami once asked me what the 'P' in her name stood for because she would always sign her name "P. Merle Wade". I told her that it stood for "Paloma", which is the Spanish translation for "dove". Mami thought was the most beautiful name and said that she was truly God sent. Their long distance friendship and sisterhood lasted until Merle's passing on May 18, 2014. Mami was so sorry to hear about P. Merle and prayed for her daughter Karen and was glad that I was able to make it to New Jersey to pay my final respects to Paloma, as she preferred to call her.

Mrs. Clara:

Mrs. Clara and Mami met at St. Andrews Catholic Church when Mami moved to Indianapolis. They became instant friends because of their love for playing Scrabble and the Lord. They played often and scheduled dates to do so. We thought it was so cute. They both created their own words and we let them do whatever they wanted. Mrs. Clara is 90 years old and who is going to argue with her about the words she and Mami made up that we could not find in the dictionary. Besides playing word games, they went to plays and church together. Mrs. Clara, who still drives, would come pick Mami up to go places and just come over to spend the day with her. They developed such a bond that it was so touching to see. When Mami moved to Indianapolis, we knew that it would be best for her care, as she got older.

But, we worried about taking her away from the strong friendships that she had forged and maintained in Panama. I personally worried about her being able to connect with people her age in a totally new environment, knowing that we controlled her whereabouts and my sister and brother-in-law worked, so were limited with getting her out. But, Mami managed to do her magic at connecting. Mrs. Clara was introduced to her and they clicked. At times, they would go to church on their own and Mrs. Clara would get there so early because she drove slowly. That drove Mami crazy, but she still rode with her and got up much earlier than normal when she knew she was riding with her. Because it would take her longer to arrive to the church. We thought that was so funny because Mrs. Clara would arrive and we would have to rush Mami to get ready and not have her waiting for her. Mami went along with the program. I remember when Mami would spend the summers with me, she would call Mrs. Clara every day to check on her and at times Mrs. Clara would beat her to it. But they spoke everyday while apart. Mrs. Clara lives in an assisted living ranch style home. For the Christmas holidays of 2016, we took Mami to spend a day with her and Mami told us that they ate some soup, played a few games and then both took a nap. Telling Mrs. Clara of Mami's death was hard. She was so sad. She had lost her Scrabble partner, her buddy, her dear friend. She expressed how she missed talking on the phone with Mami and spending time with her.

As I wrote this chapter and shared with my baby sister Maritza some of the experiences these amazing women from Mami's sisterhood shared, she asked if I wasn't going to include any males. My initial response was no because the chapter was about "Sisterhood". But, it kept tugging at me that Mami had some excellent male friends and I needed to mention them in particular Carl Clark, who wrote us the most beautiful letter of sympathy. I have included the letter in the following pages for you to read also. His penmanship reminded me of Mami's. Back then it was important for you to be able to write in cursive and they took classes to learn how to. Both my parents had beautiful handwriting.

There are two other male friends that Mami had that we got a chance to experience. One is Teofilo, who was an old boyfriend and she kept in touch with him over the years. I remember Teo coming to visit Mami when he would come back to Panama. Teo left to live in the United States much prior to Mami. They also kept in touch via letters and phone calls. Unfortunately Teo is not doing very well health wise and I was not able to communicate with him while doing this project. But I remember him. He was very handsome and polite. Next is Valentino Edwards, who is Neva's husband. Mr. Edwards, as we would call him has been a permanent fixture in our lives. He and Mami became friends before we were born because of his connection to Neva. Over the years, they became very close. Mr. Edwards has the best sense of humor. He loves to imitate others and make fun of them. He seems not to age in my eyes. He keeps himself up fairly well for his age. He keeps a high top fade afro on his head and dyes his gray until this day. He was the first auxiliary male nurse I had ever met. I always thought the nursing field was only for women until I met him. One vivid memory of Mr. Edwards and myself is when I fell and cut my right thumb and needed stitches. A few days later, he came by to see me and saw that my hand was really swollen and sensitive. He told Mami something was really wrong and she needed to take me back. He was so right. My hand was infected and I required wound debridement because of it. He pretty much saved my hand and I was grateful for that. Mami never forgot his birthday and would always call him. He appreciated that and said it to me when he called to express his condolences. He said that he was going to miss her phone call in July. That brought tears to my eyes. He also apologized for taking a week to call. But, he said he just could not talk because he was in such shock and grief and he needed to get himself together before calling me. That brought even more tears to my eyes. This was another person that Mami had touched so deeply and it was very clear how hurt he was as we spoke on the phone.

In the following pages, I have included Carl Clark's letter where he briefly explains who he is and what Mami meant to him.

memo from ...
Carl Clark

4/5/17

Dear Maritza:

It is regret and a deep sense of sorrow to learn of the passing of your beloved mother Jean. I pray that God will grant you and all of your family the strength to overcome the grief of your mother's passing.

I never met you, but I met your sister Angel in Atlanta many years ago. I later met your sister Francine when I traveled to Sanoma about ten years ago when I went to my stepmother's funeral. The last time I saw your mother was on this trip and was prior to your grandmother's passing.

Your mother and I were
schoolmates, neighbors,
and she was a dear
friend. We knew each
other for over 60 years
and kept in touch by
phone calls primarily
after she joined you
and your family in
the U.S. We even lived
across the street from
each other in the former
Canal Zone town of
La Boca.

I know she will be
sadly missed by your
family and a host of
many friends including
me. Please express
my condolences to your
sisters and your aunt
whom I haven't seen in
many years. God grant
her eternal peace & rest.
Sincerely, Carlyle Clark

We called most of the women in Mami's sisterhood "Tia", which means "Aunt" in Spanish. We considered them Mami's sisters also. We didn't see it any other way. Each one of these women, with the exception of P. Merle (RIP) wrote us beautiful notes upon Mami's death to express their sympathy, but mainly to let us know what Mami meant to them. The common word used to describe Mami by each was "best friend" and "sister". They all considered Mami to be their best friend and sister and this is testament of what I have seen from Mami also. She spread love evenly across her sister/ friends like she did with us. She made them each feel special and even after she left Panama, she kept close ties with each of them. Mami did not allow that physical distance to create any wedges between the lifelong bonds that she worked so hard to forge and keep. I have always admired these friendships and have always said that I wanted to be like Mami in that respect. I want to have friends for life like Mami did.

Mami taught me the biggest lesson in "Sisterhood", which I have learned and applied well. I have created bonds with women across the world. Bonds that are helping me cope with the loss of Mami. Besides my siblings, I have sorority sisters (Kinna, Wanda, Leslie, Brenda, LaQuanda, Erika and Chandra) that I make sure to see every time I go to New Jersey to check in with my boss. We made a lifetime commitment to serve our communities and support each other as women and we do it well. Mami met all of these women and she loved them. There are two women in particular that I am fused with forever, as I am G-Mama to all three of their kids that is Fiona and Chavela. These two are also my sorority sisters. I would trust them with my life, as they have entrusted me with all their kids. I also have my crew from my *Worship with Friends* group that check on me and are always open to converge on my home, as long as I am cooking. The ladies of my church family (Pastor Hale, Rev. Branch, Mrs. Annie and Angela) are also part of my support system that I can always count on. There are several more that I can always count on (Ma Shirley, Toy, Renee Collins, Shelia, Marisol, Marianna, Mable, Ron, Randy and Kenya). I am surrounded by great women and men too. I have created that sisterhood beyond bloodlines like Mami and I am proud of it. Because it is a way that Mami will live on through me.

Proverbs 27:9 "The heartfelt counsel of a friend is as sweet as perfume and incense." (NLT). A friend is like an answered prayer. My Mami was more than a friend to these women. She was their sister for life. This is proof that God answers prayers. ***#Sisterhood #Friendship***

In Loving Memory of

Paloma Merle Wade

August 11, 1939 - May 18, 2014

Foto Magia Photography

"Old friends pass away, new friends appear. It is just like the days. An old day passes, a new day arrives. The important thing is to make it meaningful: a meaningful friend or a meaningful day"

—Dalai Lama

17 A friend loves at all times, and a sister is born for a time of adversity

—Proverbs 17:17 New International Version (NIV)

Traveling Experiences

OUR FIRST TRIP with Mami was to New Orleans, Louisiana, in February of 1977. We boarded a flight for the first time in our lives. Mami and her three daughters were escorted to the airport by the entire family and friends entourage. I remember everyone being so excited for us. It was a Braniff Airlines flight and back then you had the escalators to the planes and the photographers that would take your picture as you went up the stairs and waived back at the crowd that was there to see you leave. Although, we flew coach, we got first class treatment courtesy of Papi's boss, who made a phone call to the airline and told them we were on the flight. For our first experience, it was an amazing one. They brought Mami a rose and gave us games to play with. We noticed that they did not do that with all passengers and we wondered why. We found out why when we returned and we thanked Mr. Berger for his connections and his thoughtfulness. He knew how much effort Papi had put into saving to make this happen for us and he wanted the experience to be memorable and it was because I just relived it as I wrote this paragraph.

We arrived in cold New Orleans. Cold to our standards coming from Panama. Tia Lois had coats for us and that was our first experience with winter. We were amazed about the condensation that escaped from our mouths and we pretended to be smoking. Mami would look at us and just smile. I remember the following day we looked outside and it was sunny, but we did not realize it was also cold. For us, sun meant heat or warmth. We went outside and quickly returned back inside. Tia Lois and Uncle June laughed at us. But we came back and put our new coats on and went back out to experience the surroundings.

Tia Lois and Uncle June took us to our first Mardi-Gras parade and it was exciting. We had been to carnival parades in Panama. But nothing like this. Mami just watched us and laughed. I remember the joy on her face as we experienced all that this trip had to offer. Once again, Mami and Papi made it happen for us. For several weeks we attended parades night after night and we gathered an entire luggage of beads and toys to take back to Panama. While in New Orleans, Mami and her sisters got the bright idea for us take a trip cross country to visit her other sister in California. Therefore, they made reservations on the Grey Hound bus line and we traveled for over two days, just Mami and her daughters, through Texas, New Mexico, Arizona and then California. We loved it. We got to see this country from the ground level.

As we traveled through New Mexico, we stopped in Albuquerque to pick up more passengers. A Hispanic couple boarded the bus, but there was only one seat left. They proceed to speak in Spanish plotting to speak to the bus driver to have my baby sister sit in Mami's lap to free a seat. Little did they know that we all understood everything they were saying and before they could finish their plot, Mami jumped up and told them that she paid for that seat and her child was not going anywhere. That couple got off the bus so quickly. They passed "Go" without collecting their $200. We laughed so hard after that because we knew Mami and we knew it was coming.

When we arrived at the bus station in California my Tia Brenda and Tio Lucho were there to receive us. What they had in store for us would be so amazing that we would never forget. We also connected with my big sister Francie's Godfather, who lived in Los Angeles. Tio Tomas was Papi's best friend and he joined in hosting us for an unforgettable trip. A trip that any child would dream about. We went to Magic Mountain, Disneyland and Sea World. We went to Chinese Theater, Rodeo Drive, we saw the Hollywood sign. We went to the San Diego Zoo. We did it all in California. We felt so special and we thanked Mami for bringing us cross country. As I got older and moved to the United States, I really appreciated what she did, by taking that long trip with us in a country that she was not familiar with. But she took the risk leaning on her faith and hovering over us to protect us all the way back and forth. Upon returning to New Orleans, we had stories after stories to tell. We could not wait to go back to Panama. We felt like little "Big Shots", we had been all over the United States on our first trip outside of Panama.

The New Orleans summer trips continued for many years to come. We ventured to different parts of Louisiana to visit Mami's friends and also went to Mississippi and Alabama on road trips with Tia Lois for weekend getaways. Mami was just so open and ready to go with the flow that it allowed us to experience so much at such a young age and in such short periods of time.

When the opportunity was presented for me to get a basketball scholarship at Xavier University in New Orleans, I did not hesitate and Mami was my biggest cheerleader. She encouraged me to go for it and I did. New Orleans was our second home and it was just a natural next step because I had Tia Lois there to support me. Therefore, I accepted and Mami traveled with me to enroll, along with my baby sister Maritza. I started school in the spring of 1985, given that the school years did not synch up with school year in Panama. Mami ensured that I had everything I needed to move into the dorm and money for any incidentals. They dropped me off and went back across the river to the Westbank where Tia Lois lived. While she was still in New Orleans, Mami came to visit very often on campus. When Mami left me to go back to Panama, I was sad to see her leave. But, I knew I had to make her proud by succeeding and I did. Mami continued to visit for many years until she got sick, battled and survived uterine cancer. She was a fighter and a survivor.

Upon Papi's death, Mami continued to travel throughout the United States with Abuela. Abuela lost her sight due to glaucoma. But it did not stop them, they visited Tia Brenda in Phoenix, Tia Lois in New Orleans, Tia Janet in Philly and myself in Plainfield, New Jersey. I would drive them into New York to see Tio Joe. We would gather at my home in Jersey and invite everyone. I took Mami and Abuela to see the Statue of Liberty and the World Trade Center. We have a photograph of them sitting on the Jersey side and the towers in the background. We went to see the Liberty Bell in Philadelphia. Mami and Abuela loved traveling together. When my sister

Maritza graduated from Xavier and got married, she moved to Chicago and had purchased a townhome. Mami and Abuela went to Chicago together and Maritza took them sightseeing all over town. Although Abuela could not see, we described things to her and she seemed to enjoy just being with Mami wherever she took her. I decided to move to Stone Mountain, Georgia and Maritza moved to Indianapolis. So now Mami and Abuela had new places to explore with us. My home in Stone Mountain became the gathering place and still is. As soon as Mami and Abuela came into town from Panama, family converged onto Georgia to see them. I would drive them from Georgia to Indiana and they loved it. Just going through Tennessee and Kentucky was so scenic and peaceful. That drive was so easy with passengers that just enjoyed being in the moment and went with the flow.

After Abuela died in April, 2008, Mami had lost her US permanent resident status. Since I had become a citizen, I applied to sponsor her once again. All the paperwork took a year to go through and a year later she was able to travel. She came to Georgia and Tio Joe was now living with me. We all traveled to Indiana together. We sang old Panamanian songs as we drove for eight hours and it made the ride seem so short. Mami was now in a back and forth pattern between the United States and Panama. She did not officially move until 2012 when we sold the house in Panama and my sister Francie moved to Stone Mountain with me.

A decade ago, we began taking "Spring Break" trips with the grandkids. Panama was the place of choice. I have a timeshare at the Royal Decameron resort. Mami loved it when we all came into town to visit for Spring Break. Although, Panama was a preferred location, a few years we decided to go to Phoenix to visit Tia Brenda. Mami was able to see the Grand Canyon and was so excited about that. We also went to Sedona and the landscape was amazing.

Besides traveling within the United States, Mami also traveled to Montego Bay, Kingston, and Ocho Rios in Jamaica when my sister Maritza got married in 1998. For her eightieth birthday in 2015, we took her to Rome, Italy and it was a trip of a lifetime. Once again, she was traveling with her three daughters. But this time around, Mami was being taken care of by her girls and not the other way around. Mami's face when we got to Rome was priceless. We flew overnight and arrived early morning.

She showed no signs of being tired, just excitement. We had a tour of the Vatican Museum scheduled for the following day. We woke up early, had breakfast and headed over. We were staying less than two blocks from the Vatican. We did the Vatican Museum tour and took lots of pictures. We had dinner and ate some gelato every night. Mami had a bad knee. But for this week in Rome, she never complained about any pain she just enjoyed her trip. The following day we took the hop-on hop-off bus to tour around the city and see the different sights. We went shopping down Milan Ave. and came back with bags and souvenirs for all of her friends. We bought leather goods at very reasonable prices. We ate pizza and beer for lunch and gelato that night. We went to Sunday mass at St Peter's square. We got there early enough to get a good seat. We anxiously waited for mass and we watched on the big screens that are set up outside. But, what we really wanted was to see Pope Francis. We were told that he could make an appearance in the Pope mobile through the crowd or come to the window. Well, the Pope made his appearance via a window and he blessed the crowd. I looked over at Mami at that moment and the grin on her face said it all for me. I knew that was the best birthday gift we could have given her. That was the trip that she was waiting for. She came back from that trip and she called everyone she knew to tell them about her trip and what her daughters had done for her at eighty years old. She talked about the trip for many months to come and having the photo book to relive the trip allowed for all of us to go back to those moments very often. I ordered two books, one for Mami and another for my sister Maritza to have on her coffee table. When Mami passed I asked Maritza to give me Mami's copy to have for my home.

Prior to her Rome trip, I took Mami to Panama in May, 2015 for Mother's Day. Just Mami and I. I was able to spend an entire week with her and my Godmother Neva in her environment. I took Mami, Neva and Yiniva to dinner one night to a typical Panamanian restaurant in Casco Viejo named "Diablicos". We walked around a historic area and they reminisced on their childhood and times that they spent in that area. It filled my heart with joy to watch them that night. During that trip, I remember taking a ride with Mami to show her all the changes in the city. As I drove, she pointed out places that she visited when she lived there and how things had changed or no longer existed. She was amazed to see how her country had changed over the years and grown in certain areas. We also went back to see our home, which was now some type of business. There isn't much of zoning codes in Panama. We stopped to chat with the neighbors and exchanged embraces. We also went to the fish market and fresh market to get ingredients for a homemade soup that Neva was going to make for us. That was fun to do because it brought back many memories for Mami. She would go to the market all the time to get the fresh veggies to make Sunday dinner.

The next big trip that Mami took was in March-April of 2016 to celebrate her son-in-law, Alan's 50th birthday in Panama. We had a surprise party for him during our annual Spring Break trip. We had a total of twenty family and friends join us that year, plus the local crew. It was an amazing celebration Panamanian style and Mami was in the midst of it. Her friends all came out to join in the festivities and she felt right at home. We had a blast in Panama celebrating Alan in March. Then in July, I decided to have a pool party to celebrate my 50th birthday early, since I would be traveling on my actual birthday in August to Panama. Mami took that drive with my baby sister Maritza and her family back to Georgia for the pool party. She mingled and had a good time with all my friends. They all knew who she was as she sat at the table enjoying the celebration. I gave thanks to God that day for Mami giving me life when I looked at her. A life that I had made it successfully to half a century, thanks to her.

By the end of 2016 we began planning our Spring Break 2017 trip. My extended brother Ron decided to take the lead and planned it for the Bahamas this time. For months we planned and paid for our airline tickets. Tia Lois and a family friend, Cora decided to join us this year. We arrived in Nassau on March 29th, 2017 and we had a wonderful day. We walked the property and saw the beautiful aquarium and casino. Mami was so excited to be there. I looked at her and said "you made it to the Bahamas" and she smiled and looked at me and responded "yes I did". She had a t-shirt on that read "I can do all things" with some wings at the bottom. We stopped and took pictures, as we walked the property. Mami was the star, everyone took pictures of her as she posed with the Atlantis Tower behind her. Little did we know, it would be the last photograph of Mami alive. We went back to the lobby and had a night cap drinks and laughed until we got tired and retired to our rooms. Later on that night, I heard knock on the door and came to see what was going on. Mami was not feeling well so we went to her room to attend to her. She complained of nausea, but kept saying she did not know how to explain how she felt. We sat her up and gave her a ginger ale because she had been vomiting. She made it through the night and woke up the next morning weak, so we got her some breakfast and told her to relax while we went for a walk. An hour later, I got a message from my nephew urging me to come back to the room. Mami had transitioned in the Bahamas. What a beautiful place God chose for her to see last. The next couple of days were difficult. But, as a family, we got through them.

My love for travel began with Mami exposing me cross-country through the United States. I travel for a living and I have lived in many different countries. I love to travel and my extra dollars are always allocated to my travel budget. One habit that I picked up along the way of my travels was to pick up a rosary from different countries for Mami. It started when I was living in Mexico. I visited the Basilica and got a beautiful rosary that was made from crushed rose petals. When you opened the case, you would smell the scent of roses. It was beautiful and I could not wait to give to Mami. Of course, she loved it. Then as I went along the way, I picked up more rosaries in either different countries or cities. The one I got in India held a special place in her heart because she was not aware that there was such a big Catholic population in India. It was a surprise to me also. The largest one I picked up in Chile and she hung it on her wall in her bedroom. I have one in my room also. As I returned to Chile, she would ask me to bring more of those back to give out as gifts and I did.

One thing that many of my friends have said to me over the years, is that they admired how we took Mami everywhere we went. Mami was also willing to go, which was important. She was open to see and try new things. Mami was able to travel all over the United States for many years and she enjoyed everywhere she went. She was always grateful for the opportunity to get out and visit family and friends. We are glad that we had the opportunity to take her along with us for so many years. We have no regrets!!! *#Travel*

Becoming "Grandma"

MAMI'S SECOND GREATEST joy was becoming a Grandmother. She experienced this for the first time on May 10th, 2000, when Alan Oscar Johnson was born. Named after his father and his maternal Grandfather. Her first grandchild and he was a boy! Mami, Abuela and Yiniva were there in Chicago with my baby sister Maritza when "AJ" was born. I recall Mami calling to tell me that he was here and laughing at Alan because he was concerned about his new baby's head. During the delivery, they had to use the suction cups to pull him out and it made his head look like a cone. Alan, his dad, came out of the delivery room and said "he has a cone head". He was so concerned about his baby's head being deformed. For the days to follow, he would rub his head and try to mold it. Eventually, his head went back to normal shape and to date, he has a perfectly round head. We still laugh about Alan's reaction when he first saw him.

Mami was so excited to have a boy to care for. She had raised three girls and now she had the little boy she always wanted. His skin was golden and had a head full of hair. He was a good baby and had great appetite. But, he never liked breast feeding. My sister had to pump because he never caught on to it and seemed to be afraid of her breast every time she approached him with them. He had his preference and it was the bottle.

Abuela and Mami all indulged in the presence of the new baby. I took the next flight to Chicago to go meet my first nephew and it was an amazing feeling to see him. Mami was Maritza's biggest support. She did everything possible to make it easier for Maritza to care for AJ. She changed diapers, rocked him to sleep and helped bathe him. Mami was in love with this little one and it showed on her face. We took pictures of him as often as possible. He was a handsome and beautiful baby. AJ as a toddler was very active and we had to watch him. He broke his arm at two years old, he split his nose at three years old. He was all boy at an early age. He was like a little monkey, jumping all over the furniture and jumping off stairs and chairs. It was a first for Mami to see this and she was always running behind him trying to get him to slow down. Fortunately, he was very tough and did not do much crying when he fell or hurt himself.

I recall the first time AJ went to Panama for a Christmas and it was his first Christmas. AJ's paternal grandparents came with us to Panama and it was hot as heck. AJ enjoyed the heat with all of us. He spent his first Christmas in Mami's birthplace. She was excited to have us all there and her first grandchild. It was a celebration and all her friends came by to meet him. They dauted over him and brought gifts for him. It was a wonderful time with family and a new baby. Mami was overjoyed to host us.

Mami and Abuela returned to the United States when it got warmer for their usual 3-4 month stay. A few years later, Maritza and Alan had moved to Indianapolis. They had built a beautiful home in the Oakland Hills sub-division. AJ adjusted to his new home quickly. He had a big backyard and lots of space to run around. Mami loved it, she was right there to watch him as he grew up in his new home. AJ and Abuela would play together while she was seated in her favorite yellow leather chair. Mami would feed them both and take care of everything in the household while his parents went to work. Mami was running the household and she knew and liked it. She was taking care of her first grandchild like Abuela did for us. I quickly saw Mami's influence on AJ. One of Mami's favorite words was "shit". She never cursed any more than that. But, this one would roll off her tongue quickly. As kids we knew not to repeat, unless you wanted to get into trouble. Well, I guess Mami had been saying it around AJ. I remember passing by his room as he played with some of his toys. He was building something and it fell. Sure enough, the next word out his mouth was "shit" and we all knew where he got it from. I walked away and chuckled with Mami about it. We did not make a deal out of it. But Mami, made sure to watch what she said around him from there on out.

Almost three years later, on January 8th, 2003, Jalen Edward Johnson was born. Like AJ he had golden brown skin and lots of hair. But, his demeanor was mellower. By now, Maritza was an expert at being a Mom and knew what to do. But, Mami was right there once again to support her with Jalen's arrival. I also took the next flight out to meet my second nephew. It was so cute to see AJ trying to hold him and kiss him. It reminded me of my big sister Francie and me. She would tell everybody I was "her baby". AJ did the same with Jalen. They are three years apart just like my siblings and me. Maritza had spaced them out exactly like Mami did with us. Enough time in between to allow to have their own friends, but also still be close to each other, as brothers. AJ and Jalen did everything together. Mami would come visit every summer until the winter season began and she would return to Panama for the warmth.

As the boys grew older and became of school age, Mami would help them with homework, she would clean up after them and straighten their rooms and play area. She washed their clothes and folded them perfectly. She also knew where each piece of clothing was to be placed and she did. Mami was so essential to those crucial early learning years. She was also there to care for them during the summers and they would not require day care. Therefore, it was a savings for my sister for several months.

AJ was accepted to Forest Glenn Elementary school in Indianapolis. A Spanish immersion school, meaning that Spanish was the language that they would learn in. Similar to the school we went to in Panama. It was great. This was a school that required a lottery to be admitted and he got in. When it was Jalen's turn to be registered for elementary school, he was accepted by default because he had a sibling already attending the school. Mami helped them both with their Spanish homework from elementary to middle school. By then, they were both fluent in Spanish. They could now read and write it perfectly and practiced with her. She was so proud of them.

Both of the boys played little league baseball and Mami attended many of their games. She loved it because baseball was that one sport that she understood very well. Papi played and loved baseball. Papi met and played with Tommy Lasorda in Panama when the Dodgers would do the spring training in Panama. The little league baseball went on for years until they outgrew it. AJ turned to taekwondo, but he kept his love for baseball and made the team in high school. The summer of 2017 after Mami died, AJ's baseball team at Cathedral High School won the state championship and went undefeated (29-0) for the entire season. Jalen really got into basketball and plays for an AAU traveling team and also for his middle school team. Jalen's middle school team, Fall Creek Middle School, also went undefeated that same season (18-0) and he was invited to a recognition ceremony on June 26th, 2017 with the superintendent of the district. Mami continued to support them in their sports and also with ensuring they got out to school on time. Mami would get up and ensure they were up and getting ready. She would help with making their breakfast and make their beds after they left for school. They never left the house without getting their blessing from Mami.

Mami was also a very important factor in their faith and them joining the serving team at St. Andrews. I recall when each of them made their first communion and how proud Mami was of both of her boys. When they began to serve at church, she would be so proud to see them come down the aisle and be at the altar. That meant so much to her. For Mami, becoming a "Grandma" was the pinnacle. First, she finally had the boys she never had. She lived with them and was able to instill her faith and values in them. They are great students and athletes, which made her so proud. Mami's joy would overflow when she spoke of them to her family and friends. Mami would say that her "grandsons did this" and her "grandsons did that" and she would go on and on about them.

Christmas was always great because Mami would go all out for the boys. Whatever they asked for from her, they got. She played the Santa Claus role with Maritza very well. Mami was an expert at this role and taught her well. As the boys got older, their gift requests got more expensive and the list got shorter. But, Mami felt like since they were good students, they earned the gifts and I agreed. For all of us, education was first and since the boys understood that, we rewarded them at Christmas time. Being "Grandma" also meant she would cover for them and come to their defense. I watched her protect them and intercede for them with their parents. She had a soft spot for them and they knew it. They had one for her also. They would look out for her as she came up the stairs because they knew she had a knee issue. They would ask her if she needed anything and were so willing to get it for her. If they saw her headed upstairs with the laundry basket, one of them would come get it from her.

I loved watching Mami interact with the boys and live under the same roof with them because I too had that same experience. I grew up in the household with my maternal grandparents and it was amazing having them there. So, I wanted the same for my nephews and I was glad to see them have that experience, which I know as they get older they will cherish for the rest of their lives. So many of my friends did not grow up with their grandparents and had to travel to go see them, whenever they could. For me this was a blessing and I did not know it at that time. But, when I realized it, I would wish it upon any child.

Mami was not only a "Grandma" to her biological grandchildren, she served this role also with my godchildren. Since she and I took the godparent role very seriously, she looked at my godchildren as her own grandchildren. She kept up with them when she came to visit me. I would take her to see the ones that lived here in Georgia and they called her "Abuela". She liked that. She enjoyed being around them and for Christmas she would also send money for me to spoil them on her behalf. I could tell that Mami was really enjoying her role as a "Grandma". This is why in her obituary I listed all her grandchildren and extended grandchildren too. Because that is how she would have wanted it. ***#Grandma #Abuela***

Moving to United States

ABUELA DIED IN April of 2008 and Mami moved to United States in May, 2009 to establish residency in Indianapolis. Meaning that she could not be outside of the United States for more than six months. Otherwise, she would lose her "Resident Alien" status. I have always hated that name for permanent residents. It is so ugly and stigmatizes a population that pays taxes just like citizens of this country. There was no doubt or debate as to whom Mami would live with. My sisters and I knew that she wanted to help with the raising of her grandsons, just like Abuela did for us growing up in Panama. So she came to Georgia first and I drove her along with her big brother Tio Joe, who was living with me at the time, to Indianapolis. It was such a wonderful drive because we listened to old Panamanian songs and I indulged in watching them reminisce on things they did as children and places that they went to. Music has a way of taking us back to those moments and it did just that during that eight hour drive.

Mami arrived and got settled into Maritza's home. She already had a room because she visited often. But, now she was going to make it her new home. My other sister Francie remained in Panama and held down the fort while Mami was living dual lives. She was in the United States for six months and then six months in Panama. She left during winter in Indianapolis. She had the best of both worlds and she enjoyed it. Mami stayed in touch with her friends in Panama very often via email and phone calls. She was not about to let the strong bonds that she worked so hard to forge dwindle. She also wrote letters, because she loved to write. She had great penmanship, as oppose to me. My handwriting is atrocious.

Mami began to make her mark by making friends with the neighbors. Peter, who lived right next door had a beautiful garden and Mami would go pick his roses and bring them back. Peter had given her permission to do so. Across the street was Lynn, another neighbor who also knew Mami. The kids in the neighborhood knew her as AJ and Jalen's grandmother. The kids often played at my nephew's home and Mami would keep order, as she did for us in Panama. Her grandchildren loved having her there for such long periods of time.

Back in 2001, I had applied to sponsor my big sister Francie for her residency. It got approved, but the instructions stated that a sibling visa would take about ten years before it was issued and it did. Ten years later, I got notification that it was time to continue the process and we did. Therefore, we made the decision to put the house in Panama up for sale. As long as Mami went back and forth to Panama, I was ok with it. As time went by and it became evident that she should not be traveling alone and the sale of the house was more confirmation that things needed to change permanently. Mami headed back to help with all the paperwork to complete the sale. She also started with the packing of the house and I came down to assist her. We held a patio sale and sold most electronics very quickly. Sold the furniture and gave away heirloom pieces to close family and friends. We decided what trash was and what we would keep in Panama until further notice. We stored somethings at my Godmother's house. We still have some items stored at friends and family and we need to find a way to get them to the United States. These are items that hold sentimental value and we want to keep them, such as a portrait of Mami and her grandsons. The sale completed and Mami was ready to return to the United States, her permanent residency now. Mami now knew this was it. This is where she would be for the remainder of her life, with her daughters close by and her grandchildren. Just like she wanted it.

For me it was difficult seeing Mami leave her friends, so I know it was extremely hard for her too. But, her sisterhood was very supportive because they knew how important this move was for her. It was important for her to be able to contribute to the upbringing of her grandsons and be very close to her daughters. Therefore, they supported and encouraged her to go with the promise that she would come back to visit and they would come to visit her also. Over the years Mami returned at least once a year to Panama with us for Spring Break and we had a blast. My Godmother Neva came to visit also. So she got to see her several times during a year's timeframe. Mami made it a point to call very often and offered to pay for her long distance phone calls. But, we never accepted. We knew how important it was to her to keep these bonds and we supported that.

Mami then started to plant new seeds in the United States by meeting people like Mrs. Clara, The Carrolls and many others at St. Andrews church. She traveled through the United States with us to visit family. She spent the summers in Georgia with me and her grandsons. We had a summer ritual. Maritza and Alan would pack their bags and drive to the midpoint between Stone Mountain and Indianapolis, which was Nashville. We had a spot, a Japanese restaurant. We met in the parking lot and had lunch. I would take my sister's SUV and she would take my car. I would keep Mami and the kids for about 4-6 weeks, then my sister would drive my car down to pick them up and spend a week in Georgia with me. We looked forward to it every summer until the kids got older and weren't too keen on spending the summers with their auntie anymore. Now they came, but at most for two weeks. I still went up to visit Mami for holidays because family is always first in my book.

When Mami got her residency, Maritza made sure that she had medical support and got doctors to treat her asthma. Maritza knew what to do to ensure Mami was under the necessary care and she gave her the best care possible for the rest of her life. In fact, Maritza is who led the paramedic's team in the Bahamas to try to resuscitate Mami. It was amazing to see her at work and to be so calm while I was in crisis. I am forever thankful for her skills and her attempt.

Now that Mami was in the United States for good, she adapted very quickly. That was just her personality. She fit right into the household. She had her daily chores that she performed like washing/folding clothes, being the sous chef, watering the plants, cleaning up after the boys and helping with homework. Mami enjoyed her responsibilities and she executed her tasks very well. Alan, her son-in-law, loved having her in the house. Their relationship was unusual. They laughed a lot and never had any disagreements. They sat up and had many beers together on Saturday nights. He often fired and rehired her, when her chores were not done. We would laugh every time we heard him say "Jeannie you're fired", she thought that was so funny and the next morning he would rehire her again. Mami really didn't need to do any chores. But these kept her feeling like she belonged to the household and she wanted to contribute. So they let her. She did the same thing when she came to visit me for the summers. She would look for things to do and laundry was always the main thing. She enjoyed folding the clothes, as she watched "Wheel of Fortune", "Jeopardy" or "Family Feud". Mami enjoyed most game shows and watching CNN to stay on top of the latest news.

Life in the United States became the norm for her and she adapted to all the season changes. She would always tell us about her father singing the Christmas song, "White Christmas" and she never thought she would ever see a White Christmas while growing up. Her dream became a reality when she moved to Indianapolis. Her body adjusted to the season and soon she grew to like the cold winters in Indianapolis. Of all seasons, she loved the fall the most. Mami enjoyed watching the leaves change colors and fall off the trees. Maritza would take Mami to take pictures under a tree at the entrance of their subdivision every October. We called it her pre-birthday photoshoot. Then we would post the pictures on Facebook on her birthday in November. By November, the leaves were all on the ground and the tree was bare, so we had to take the pictures in October.

Moving Mami to the United States to be closer to her daughters and sisters was the best decision we made for her and we are also glad that she was open to doing it and loved her new environment. If we had to do it all over again, we would do it the same way we did it before. *#NoRegrets #Panama #Indianapolis*

"Travel and change of place impart new vigor to the mind.

—Seneca

Live 2 Give

A
S A CHILD, I watched how my Mami's giving spirit just overflowed from her. She was always giving someone something. It started as a child, she shared her toys with her best friend Neva. Her vast collection of paper dolls and kitchen set too. Mami lived her life to give. She discovered it was the key to a successful spiritual life. Sometimes she gave when she really did not have. So, she gave her last knowing that God would provide for her. Mami walked by faith and not by sight. (2 Corinthians 5:7).

When my parents decided to build a home in Rio Abajo, Panama they knew it was not the most affluent area. But, it was part of their roots and my GrandDaddy had the land in this location. My parents built a five bedroom home that was about 2,500 square feet. It had a huge garage or carport area and beautiful yard. It was built by a friend of the family, Architect Smith. I went to school with his daughter and his wife was my Geography teacher. We moved in on May 1st, 1970, Labor Day. My baby sister Maritza was just a few months old. We quickly made friends with the surrounding neighbors. Our neighbors did not have much. My parents built, what the rest of the people in the neighborhood, at that time, considered to be a mansion. Everyone wanted to play in our yard and we let them. Mami became very close with the neighbor in the back, Sra. Lupe and also next door, Sra Lala. I recall looking out my window very often and watching Mami hand the neighbor in the back, eggs, flour, milk and sometimes money. Just the basic needs to survive. I watched her hand it over and come back inside to finish cooking or doing her laundry. At times, she would just send me over to give them a plate of food. Mami was very aware of her surrounding neighbors and their needs. She also knew which kids in the neighborhood belong to which parents.

Mami fed all the kids in the neighborhood. It did not matter who they were. When she rang that dinner bell, if they came running home with us, she fed them. She always seemed to have enough. During the holidays in Panama, it is customary for the neighbors to exchange a plate of food. We loved how Sra. Lupe cooked and anxiously waited for her to send her plate of rice with pork and the purple potato salad. It was purple because she added beets to it. She also made the best tamales. It was not a big plate, but we all got a taste and enjoyed it very much. In exchange Mami would prepare a large plate with ham and turkey and fruit cake to share with them. Most neighbors could not afford a ham and turkey. So she made sure they got some during that time of year from her. Papi would get several ham and turkey baskets from his clients, so Mami would cook them and give it away.

Mami believed in tithing and she did. She gave to God what belonged to Him. She knew that all our possessions came from Him and she gave back willingly. She never gave expecting anything in return. She gave because it was the right thing to do. She understood this and instilled this in us. Mami not only gave food, money or things. She gave her time to listen and advise others, she gave her space in her home to house others. When we left for college Mami opened her doors to family members and close family friends to live with her, as they got their finances together. She never asked for anything in return from them. She was glad to have them there with her. To date, these friends and family members are so glad for that opportunity because it changed the course of their lives forever. Her doors continued to be opened to all until we sold our home in Panama in November, 2011.

Mami's giving spirit she inherited from her mother, Abuela. Abuela gave every family member fifty dollars on their birthday and we looked forward to it. I know I planned on what I would do with my fifty bucks every year. Mami managed Abuela's finances and distributed the fifty dollars throughout the year. She allowed Abuela to do whatever she wanted with her money. Mami followed in her footsteps by also giving the fifty dollars after Abuela died. She continued with the tradition and I loved watching her. Christmas was just a time for Mami to go bananas. She had the longest list. At times, we would ask her why she had to buy anything for certain people because we never really heard from them anymore. But, Mami insisted that she wanted to get them a gift and we let it go and just took her shopping for whomever she wanted to give a gift to. It was her way of showing her love and care and we respected that. We would drive her around to deliver gifts, as we did on many Christmas eves in Panama. It was fun and exciting. She felt like Santa Claus, a role she played very well for us when we were children.

I remember on one occasion that Mami won some money in the lottery in Panama and she gave most of it away. She spread those few thousands of dollars across anyone that came across her path. After my parents paid off the mortgage on our family home in Panama, Mami proceeded to add each of us to the deed. I did not know that until we decided to sell the home and both Maritza and I had to send letters granting Mami and Francie permission to sell the property. When the property was sold, we split the profits into four. Mami was firm that we should each get an even amount, it did not matter to her who already had what. She said one fourth for each. Mami took hers and she further spread hers to her siblings and whomever she wished. We just let her, as usual. If Mami had, it meant the people in her circle would never need and her circle was not small.

Because Mami gave so much to us and to others, we felt the need to give back to her in every form possible. We did that by giving her our time, giving her gifts, giving her trips/vacations, etc. We had to give her the rewards of her paying it forward many years prior. We took Mami everywhere we went. We gave her the best that we could and we learned from her ways.

I can say that this giving quality is something that I have inherited from Mami. For many years I would throw parties, BBQs, crab boils at my home and also entertain friends and family. I always had a big birthday party until I turned forty five. Then I decided that I would live my life with a purpose bigger than myself and I would donate my birthday to a cause. I began asking friends that in lieu of gifts for my birthday that they would bring their used clothes and shoes to donate to the homeless. I was amazed at the amount of bags that covered the floor in my living room. We could not even walk into the room. Next, I decided to have toy drive for Christmas for children in shelters and that was also a success. A few years later, I started a group named DOWAP (Dining Out With A Purpose). The idea came to me while dining with some friends. We were constantly eating and drinking out. So why not do it with a purpose of serving others. So, we discussed it and I presented them with a plan on how to accomplish our goal. I created a website and Facebook page and we approached restaurants that would allow us to come in and take-over for a few hours and in exchange they would give 20% of whatever we spend in their establishment to a charity of our choice. It was an instant success and a win-win situation for all involved. This went on for years, until my travel schedule got in the way and other members could not dedicate the needed time to it. But, we continue to have events, as often as possible. Because I was traveling so much, I decided to start collecting all the toiletries from the hotel for the homeless. Since I would bring my own toiletries. I then connected with a friend to provide her with them to distribute around the Atlanta homeless communities. As I started giving, I felt the need to give even more. I now knew why Mami did what she did. I had discovered the key to a successful life. I had discovered how to live to give. I then started a Facebook page titled "Live2Give" and it is just a space for people to post information about giving opportunities. I even had a few t-shirts printed with the logo and many have inquired about purchasing them. I need to follow up on that idea and find a charity to donate the profits to.

Upon Mami's death, we decided to give away some of her clothing, shoes, household items and jewelry. We donated it to Mission 27 downtown Indianapolis. They were so thankful for our donations. We knew that is what Mami would have wanted us to do with her things. The most precious gift that Mami gave was *unconditional love*. Mami did not judge, she just loved people in general. The people she touched have all said to us that they felt so loved by Mami. Her smile was loving, her words were loving, her food was prepared with love, her advice was loving, and her faith was loving. As her daughter, I can say that the greatest love I have ever felt came from Mami. A mother's love is the greatest gift a child can ever receive. #Live2Give

"It is possible to give freely and become wealthier…" (NLT).

—Proverbs 11:24

"One of the secrets of being happy is doing things for other people."

—MALANDA

Being Her Daughter

S THE FIRST born, Francie had the privilege of experiencing Mami longer that any of us. I must say that I am so proud to be her daughter. I have always spoken Mami's name with pride and will continue to do so because that is all I feel when I think of her. Mami was strong and courageous. Mami was a great mother, godmother, grandmother, friend, wife and sister. Mami was our biggest cheerleader. I want to be like Mami. I have learned so many lessons from her that I plan to continue to pass them down to my next generations and hopefully, anyone else open and willing to receive these lessons.

Being her daughter was super easy. She made it like that for each one of us by allowing us to be different individuals. She knew who was good at what and she pushed those strengths in each of us. Mami knew I was the athlete and the streetwise one. So she let me be outside playing all types of sports with the boys. I would play basketball all day long. I was really good at it too. Mami allowed me to play in leagues around the city. She would sometimes show her face on the balcony if things got a little too rowdy on the court. Like I said before, she heard and saw everything. The kids had much respect for her. Mami would allow all of us to come back inside and get some water from the outdoor hose and then go back to our game. She did not worry about me. Because she knew I could handle it. I thank her for that because in my line work, I deal mainly with men and work on teams. I know exactly how to handle myself with them. I think part of a mother's job is to recognize those skills in each child and do the best to enhance and encourage growth in them.

When I decided to leave for college, she never tried to stop me. She encouraged me and helped me with my application. Mami made me feel like I was making the right choice. She wanted me to go off and rise to new levels. She had prepared me my entire childhood for that moment. Playing basketball for all those years as a child paid for my entire college tuition, books and room/board. After I graduated from college, I got a job in New Jersey. As I grew professionally, I had the opportunity to travel around the world with my job. I would always share with Mami what opportunities came up for me and she would always encourage me to take them and make the best of them, with the exception of one. Back in late nineties, I had an opportunity to go work in South Africa. It was a huge project that the company was gearing up to implement. Several of my friends applied and made the teams. When I approached Mami about it, she said she did not have a good feeling about it and I did not go. Thank God I didn't because the project fell apart. The company ended up in court with the client and many came back to no jobs when they returned to the United States. I was so glad that I listened to her instinct.

To be her daughter was to experience unconditional love. It meant to feel protected by her at all time. A few days after Papi's funeral, I decided to cook and was using the pressure cooker. It malfunctioned and exploded on me. Melting my skin off on my face, left arm and my entire chest. Mami's first reaction was to dive towards me and grab me. She slipped in the hot water, but got up and came towards me. Mami dumped me into the shower and ran the cold water on me. She took all my clothing off and then asked my sister to go get the toothpaste. She always told us that toothpaste was good for burns because the cooling mint in it would take the heat out of the layer of skin. She put toothpaste all over me and calmed me down. I was in shock and in so much pain. My baby sister Maritza drove us to the nearest emergency room where Mami explained to the doctor what happened. He asked what was on my skin and she told him. He said that she saved me from having deeper burns by dumping me in the shower and putting the toothpaste on. But, that they had to clean it all off to see how severe it was and it was going to be a painful process. It was excruciating. The doctor told Mami that I would most likely need plastic surgery. They cleaned me up and then gave Mami the instructions for caring for me for the coming weeks. My care consisted of several showers a day and application of a cream. I could not wear any clothing. I just laid in bed with a light sheet covering me. A few days after this incident, I noticed Mami's arm was filled with blisters. When she fell trying to get to me, she burned her arm severely. But, her concern for me was greater than for herself. I felt so bad for her because she eventually had to go to the hospital to get it taken care of. It also left a very dark mark on her arm, which over the years cleared up some. But, every time I would see her arm I was reminded of that day and what it was like to be her daughter. It meant she would protect me by any means necessary. I was thirty years old when this happened and Mami was still doing what she did best for me and that was to nurture and love me.

In 1994, when I decided to build my first home, I was short one thousand dollars for my down payment. I had applied for an FHA (Federal Housing Administration) loan and it required a certain amount for the down payment. I called Mami and told her about it. But, I was not asking because I knew my parents didn't just have that kind of money just laying around to give me. But, Mami spoke with Papi and told him that they needed to find a way to help me because I never asked for anything. I got myself through college and master program without them having to pay anything. I bought my first car without them helping. So, she felt that this was an opportunity for them. Papi sold some of his shares at the company to get the money and Mami wired it to me. They were both so proud of me being the first to buy and build a home. Papi got the money but Mami brokered the deal for me. I am forever grateful to her for the boost of help. I offered to pay them back, but they refused, simply because I was their child.

Being her daughter meant having to deal through some very rough moments with her. When I was twelve years old a neighbor decided to reveal to me that Papi was having an affair with her sister. Who does that to a child? I ran home and knew I could not tell Mami. So I told Abuela about it because I knew she would tell her child. I felt so bad having to bring such bad news to Mami because I knew it was going to hurt her. I could not sleep that night and anxiously waited for Papi to come home to see what was going to happen. Mami closed their bedroom door and I could hear them arguing. I think Mami was more upset about the impact it would have on me as a child. She was pissed that this woman had said such a thing to her child and pissed at him for giving her anything to say. For many days and weeks to come, things were very tense in the house and I felt like it was my fault. Mami came to me and reassured me that everything was going to be fine and that I did not do anything wrong. She made me feel better because I asked her if this meant they would get divorced. She told me that she and Papi were going to work it out and they did. I must say that Mami forgave him for it and we carried on as a family. At least he knew Mami was not going to play like that with him, probably why he never told her that he had a child out of wedlock also. When Papi died in 1996, a few days after his funeral, a man approached me at my home and handed me a letter. I opened and read it out loud and it basically revealed the existence of a young lady who is Papi's daughter. Ironically, as soon as I saw a photo of this young lady the memories of her started to flash through my mind. I recalled in a matter of seconds everywhere I had ever seen her, at the funeral crying her eyes out and me wondering who she was, at the hospital waiting room, at the Burger King close to the house where Papi would always stop to get us a quick meal. It all made sense now why she was crying so hard at the funeral. Papi had told her that if there was anyone that she could tell and would understand, it would be me. So once again, I had to deliver the bad news to Mami. I felt awful. But at least this time around I was thirty years old and not twelve. Mami had a very hard time digesting this news and accepting this. I had to sit with her and my siblings and reason with them about the fact that this young lady was not at fault and that if they wanted to be upset with anyone, he was six feet under by now. It took Mami months to get over this. She went into a depression and I had to return to Panama to stay with her for some time. Luckily my boss was very flexible and allowed me to work remotely. I know that Mami's faith is what got her through that situation. Her friends and family rallied around her and covered her with love and support. That sisterhood that she had created many decades prior became her backbone. They came to Mami's rescue and uplifted her. Mami prayed a lot and cried a lot during this timeframe of her life. But, prayer won because Mami eventually accepted the situation and became an advisor to this young lady. My half-sister Ariadne told Mami that Papi spoke of her very highly and that she admired how she was raising us with so much love. Something that she did not get from her own mother. So Mami put herself aside to embrace and support her because she realized that was something that Papi would have wanted. Unfortunately, we are not close to Ariadne. But, we do keep in touch via Facebook and WhatsApp. The biggest difference in this case was that Ariadne was Papi's daughter. But we were Mami's daughters and those things did not equate because the main ingredient in our life was Mami.

I clearly remember the day I decided to tell Mami about my sexual preference. Although in the back of my mind, I already knew that she knew. She knew all of us very well. Her response was ok so what and I just cried and thanked her for accepting me. She never tried to change me or make me feel like something was wrong with me. She just wanted to protect me from other people that would try to make me feel less than who I am. That was her biggest concern with that subject. I remember growing up feeling different but not understanding why I did. Therefore, I over compensated by being excellent at everything that I did, school, sports, art work, etc. I thought that would mask my sexual preference and no one would notice it. So it made me an overachiever. That was good because it helped me excel in school. But it didn't change who I really was and eventually I realized that. Mami was cool with it and it became very important to me to expose her to my friends/community. So when I had my first real partner, Mami and Abuela would come visit us in Georgia. I would host some gatherings with my friends to expose Mami to them. I wanted her to see that my friends were just normal people and just liked to have fun. Mami already knew that. Mami welcomed each one of them. She took the time to get to know them personally. Mami became a part of our gatherings and my friends loved her. Being her daughter meant she accepted me and my friends.

When I turned thirty nine, I decided to get my first tattoo. I had a stigmatized mentality about tattoos because of all the negative things I heard growing up. It was equivalent to wearing the ankle bracelet on the wrong ankle. You could quickly get labeled. After doing some research about tattoos, I eventually got over it and decided to get one. Well, when I went back to Panama and showed Mami, she did not react one way or another, which meant she was not too pleased. I did talk to her about it and she also got over it. Simply because I was her child. She knew that a tattoo would not change me. Mami was just concerned that others would label me and mistreat me. But at the same time, she knew I could handle myself. I went ahead and got two more tattoos until Mami died. As a tribute to Mami, I got my fourth tattoo below my right wrist. I have the Japanese symbol for "Mother" inked on me and I love it. I got a lot of positive feedback from friends and family when I posted the picture on my Facebook page. They all felt like it was a great tribute and loved the significance of the tattoo. I feel like I carry Mami with me daily and everywhere I go. Mami is forever inked on me.

The one thing I miss the most about being her daughter is our daily chats. I work from home, so I called Mami all day long in between my conference calls. I kept her entertained and she kept me entertained. Mami was my first phone call of the day. Her voice was the sweetest sound to my ears. The way she would answer the phone and sing the word "hoooooolaaaaaa" would just bring a smile to my face. My siblings and I often chuckled about the way she said that word. We loved and miss hearing it. Nobody can say "hola" like Mami. Nobody!!!

As I got older Mami became more than just my mother, she became my friend. Mami knew us so well and I knew that. I knew that if I told Mami of anything that I needed my sister to do, she would make it happen, as long as she agreed with my objectives. Mami was a perfect mediator and she knew how to engage us in positive interactions to ensure that we got along, as sisters should. One of the last things Mami did for me still makes me laugh out loud. In February 2017, I decided to renovate the hall bathroom. This bathroom had wallpaper and I wanted to modernize it. I am really good at doing things myself, so I took the wallpaper down, cleaned and smoothened the walls. I painted it a beautiful light blue in semi-gloss to resist the moisture. I then changed the light fixtures, cabinet fixtures and faucets. The last step was to now decorate it with new curtains, rugs and wall décor. It was a brand new bathroom and it only took me two days. My big sister Francie came home and loved it. Therefore, I offered to do her on-suite bathroom. She looked and me and shrugged her shoulders and said no and that she was fine with the way her bathroom was. I was not very happy about her decision because all the bathrooms in the house were now updated except for hers. I decided to call Mami and tell her about Francie's decision and I also showed her pictures of the bathroom I renovated. Mami loved it and could not understand why Francie would not let me redo her bathroom. It was President's day weekend and since Francie works at the bank she was off that Monday. Francie left the house to run errands and came back with bags. Within those bags, she had a new shower curtain and new bathroom rugs. I just smiled and then came up to her room and said to her "oh you decided to update the bathroom" and she shyly said "yeah". I then said "but you really need for me to take down that wallpaper and paint the wall in a color that would really match your accessories" and she said "ok". I was shocked and in disbelief, so I rushed to Home Depot to get the paint. I began stripping the wallpaper from the wall that same afternoon and told her she should use the hall bathroom until I finished hers. That night before we went to bed, I asked her out of curiosity what changed her mind about me updating her bathroom. Francie responded, "Your Mother" and my eyes got big and I smiled. Francie then said "Mami said that when she came to visit she was not taking a shower in ugly and old bathroom and that she was going to use the hall bathroom". Mami often stayed in the room with Francie when she visited. I covered my mouth in disbelief because I could not believe how Mami's mediation efforts helped persuade my sister in updating her bathroom. I then called Mami and told her what happened and we both got a good laugh before going to bed. I told her I was in disbelief and Mami told me all I needed to do was thank her. Next day I sent pictures of the bathroom for Mami to see them and she loved it also. Mami was something else. She knew what to say and do to get us going. Unfortunately, Mami died before she could see any of the bathrooms.

Mami was blessed with so many gifts. She was an artist and could draw very well. Mami always helped us with our school projects and homework. She had a beautiful garden with lots of roses. She liked making ceramics and her house was adorned with her creations. Mami gave many of her dear friends her creations as gifts. Unfortunately, when we moved her to the United States, we had to give them away. Mami also had the gift of peace. Mami was the peacemaker and would be the mediator in most situations. Mami's voice was very soft and loving all the time. Her home was extremely peaceful. Some people would say that her home was like "sugar" you just could not get enough of it. There was always a good vibe and people would come and stay very long. But, her most precious gift was her gift of empathy. Mami had a way of being able to feel for others and put herself in their shoes. Mami had that sensibility for others. In my quest of being more like Mami, I am working on being more empathetic with others, as I go through my journey of life. Besides gifts, Mami taught me and many others, many lessons that are scattered throughout these chapters. Life lessons that I will carry on and hope will help others. Mami was considered a "Teacher of Life" and "Spiritual Counselor" by many of her friends.

I asked my big sister Francie what was it like being her daughter and this is what she said to me:

"My mother was always so good at what she did that I often believed that in every household it was the same, the norm. But, as I grew older I learned that I was very blessed for having such a beautiful and loving mother. She was always taking care of us, keeping us groomed and tidy. Mami was a fashionista and trendy. Mami kept us updated in style and hairdos. My mother designed and created such lovely dresses and costumes for each fun time event that we were ever involved in. She was an innate creator, always doing something with her hands, which was not only for creating lovely art, but for giving love to us, her daughters. Mami knew each one us and would engage each one of us at our own level of weakness and strength. I love her so dearly, but I was not one to express it much. I was more of a doer than a talker. I was very quiet and never said much growing up, but I knew and she knew that I loved her. No family is perfect, and it was not meant to be perfect. All I can say is that

my relationship with Mami was at times, argumentative, but never to the point of becoming resentful or bitter about our differences, rather it was so obvious that she was in most cases (always) right about the issue. It was just a matter of me coming to my senses and acknowledging that Mami knows best and her motherly wisdom was unsurpassable. I could never compete and win, she would always win me over with her love and understanding. I could say more, but I would like to keep the rest to myself. We ought not to have to unveil everything, for some treasures are to be kept in the depths of our hearts and soul".

I also asked my baby sister Maritza to write down what she would want to express about Mami and this is what she wrote:

"When my sister asked me to write something about "Mami" for some reason it was difficult to do it...I was still in denial that she had passed away and was no longer here with us. I wanted to believe that it was all a dream and that one day, I would wake up with a sigh of relief that it was not true!

But it is true and I wake up now reliving all the things that she embodied for years and made me whom I am today. There are five things I give thanks to the Lord for every morning when I get up and these five things represent my "Mami":

Life
She was full of life and she lived it to the fullest! She enjoyed trying new things and traveling and meeting lots of people on her way. No matter what the circumstances were she always expressed to trust in the Lord because everything happens for a reason and He will show you the right way. She was non-judgmental and would always tell me that life is a gift from God and to be thankful for everything (small and big). She loved nature and planting flowers during the spring season. I can picture her on the deck admiring all the flowers we would plant together and watch them flourish throughout the season. She had no regrets. She held no grudges and most of all, she loved being a "Mami".

Love

She was a lovely person inside and out. Everyone who met her would feel that love she radiated. From her contagious smile to her quirky statements that would make us all laugh out loud! After her passing I heard from so many people that she touched in so many ways from a simple phone call, to greeting cards, to visits she made; so many little things that made a huge difference in so many ways that only a person who expressed love could do so effortlessly.

Intelligence

Mami was full of wisdom. This is probably the hardest of all, not having her around to talk to when I'm down and not feeling well. She always knew what to say and what to do to make me feel better and smile again! Her wisdom of course was generational from Abuela and all the other elders who taught her well enough for her to pass it on. She was a very strong will and determined person. She loved helping her grandchildren with homework and even helped me study for my Nurse Practitioner certification exam.

Beauty

It goes without mentioning that her beauty was inside and out. Not only did I admire her beauty, I loved to dress her up and often refer to her as my "muñequita" which meant "my baby doll". Whenever we would go on trips she would wait for me to help her pack her outfits and her accessories because she enjoyed it as much as I did! We would schedule pedicures and hairdresser appointments together and shopping all day Saturdays!

Harmony

Mami lived a very peaceful life. She had no worries, no regrets and most of all she was at peace with God. She loved listening to her prayer channel on TV and would say her rosary two to three times a day. She lived a life of prayer. There were times that she would not be able to attend church but that didn't stop her from listening to it on the TV or radio. She would often tell me not to worry because nothing good comes from worrying; instead pray for guidance to lead you to the right path. No sense in worrying it can only bring about your downfall; wait and be patient and the situation will resolve itself. She knew that living in harmony meant peaceful living the way God intended for us to live!

These five things Mami taught me well and for that I love her and miss her very much! I wake up every morning giving thanks for life, love intelligence, beauty and harmony all the things she was and will always be to me! Te quiero mucho Mami!!!"

Being her daughter meant that you always felt love, that you would have an extended group of aunties from her solid sisterhood, that you would have seven additional brothers and sisters through God, that you did not have to call and let her know you were bringing friends home, that you could tell her anything and not feel judged, that you would always have a confidant, that you would always have a friend, that you would always feel protected and safe, that you would be encouraged when you were feeling down, that you would know she was always praying for you, that she would do anything to make you laugh even at her own expense, that she would participate in all of our buffoonery, that you would never feel alone, that you would feel stronger around her, that she would support you in whatever decisions you made, that she would teach you whatever she knew, that she would prepare you for this world, that she would walk you down the aisle on your wedding day because Papi was deceased, that there would always be food on the table, that you could be different, that you could make mistakes and that you could conquer the world just because she said so.

"Being deeply loved by someone gives you strength. Loving someone deeply gives you courage"

—LAO TZU

Foto Magia Photography

Mother's Day

MOTHER'S DAY IN Spanish is "Dia de las Madres". It is actually celebrated on December 8th in Panama. That particular date is the *"Feast of the Immaculate Conception"* and we celebrate the solemn belief in the Immaculate Conception of the Blessed Virgin Mary. It is one of the most important Marian feasts in the liturgical calendar of the Roman Catholic Church, celebrated worldwide. Our Mother's Day celebration directly correlates to the strong Catholic beliefs in the country. Panama was colonized by the Spaniards and Catholicism became the dominant religion. Mother's Day is a holiday in Panama regardless of what day of the week December 8th falls on. It is a big celebration across the country.

I recall growing up and making cards in school and proudly presenting them to Mami on that day. All three of us would march into her room early morning to bring her our cards and gifts. Papi would also have a gift for her. But, Mami would get moving early to prepare breakfast and then dinner for us. For Mami it was her day, but she knew her responsibility as a "Mother" was to ensure we had food on the table too. We would visit our Godmothers or they would visit us. We would make sure to call our Tias and acknowledge all our neighbors on that day. I would call my friend's mothers to wish them a wonderful day. When I was growing up, the stores would be closed that day and it was truly a holiday. Over the years that changed and although it is still a holiday for many, some people do work that day. As we got older, we would take Mami out to eat to celebrate her and buy her gifts.

Mami was blessed because since I moved to the United States, I began to also celebrate Mother's Day on the second Sunday in May. So she would get two wishes per year. I would also get two sets of cards in May and save one to mail to her in December. Mami was thrilled to get my cards all the way from the United States. She loved to receive mail. I was so glad that I could celebrate her twice a year. I would post on my Facebook page on both dates and would tell people the meaning of it. I lived in Mexico for four years. Mexicans celebrate Mother's Day on a fixed date also, May 10th. It is a major holiday for them also. My nephew AJ was born on that day. So that was also a default day that we would celebrate Mami in a Mexican way. My dear friend Kenya in Mexico would always send a warm message for Mami. Although she had never met her. Kenya was very fond of Mami because she knew Mami had prayed for her during some difficult moments in her life and I was living there in Mexico going through those moments with her. I shared everything with Mami and she always knew how to make it better.

At the same time I celebrated my Mami on both occasions, I made sure to celebrate all of the Mothers in my life (Godmothers, Mother-in-laws, Aunts, friends, Sorority sisters, etc.). I would take them to lunch or dinner, send cards, post on my Facebook and Instagram pages and make phone calls. I know how important it is to maintain these bonds with these women. These women have supported me over the years and Mami loved them all for being there for me. She appreciated every single one of them because I spoke of them so highly and often. Many of these women were also part of her sisterhood and she was glad to see how it extended to her off-springs.

Mami and Abuela would often come for their yearly visit from May – November. So they were in the United States for Mother's Day and AJ's birthday. They had two celebrations to participate in, as soon as they arrived in Indianapolis. My baby sister Maritza would dress them up and take them to church and then lunch or brunch with the Carrolls. They both looked forward to it and enjoyed being the center of attention. The celebration continued in this manner after Abuela died and Mami moved permanently.

At times, I would make my way up to Indiana to be part of the celebration and I loved it. Although Mami did not need to do anything on that day, she enjoyed being the sous chef for Maritza. Mami was always so willing to participate in whatever was happening in the household. She would just fit right in and go with the flow. She did that wherever she went.

I travel a lot for my job and I was on assignment in Lima, Peru in 2014. I decided to spend Mother's Day that year by visiting Machu Picchu, one of the seven wonders of the modern world. Mami was always thrilled about my travel adventures. I recall calling Mami from the top of Machu Picchu on that Mother's Day Sunday and telling her where I was standing. I can still picture the joy on her face based on the tone of her voice during that phone call. I could not wait to send pictures for her to see me. I knew she was proud of me. I posted the pictures on my Facebook page when I got back to hotel that evening and I immediately called my sister for her to show Mami. Mami loved every single picture and of course called all her family/friends to tell them about my trip. By the time, I called them they already knew I had been to the mountain top and completed seeing and experiencing my fourth wonder of world.

May 14th, 2017, was my first Mother's Day without Mami. I will not look at this as a negative because I have so many wonderful memories to celebrate her. I do not have any biological children, but I raised a beautiful child (Jasmine Noelle Smith-Brundage) from my previous partnership. A child that Mami considered her grandchild and loved dearly. Well, Jasmine became a mother for the first time on February, 24th, 2017. Although Mami never met Rilynn Noelle, she saw many pictures of her and was very proud and happy for Jasmine. I know what Mami would want me to do at this time in my life. And that is to celebrate Jasmine's first Mother's Day and not my first without her. That is exactly what I did. The day prior I went to mass at Corpus Christi Catholic Church in Stone Mountain, Georgia. On that Sunday, I went to breakfast with Jasmine and her family and we had a wonderful time. We honored Mami and spoke of her highly. I also visited Mami at Melwood cemetery to have my time alone with her after breakfast. Finally, I spent the remainder of my day with three of my eight godchildren. Overall, it was a beautiful day and I can say that I am so proud to be her daughter forever. Simply because Mami was a unique soul and we had the pleasure and honor of experiencing her. We continue to learn from her and hopefully pass along those lessons to many generations to come. *#MothersDay #DiaDeLasMadres*

28 Her children arise and call her blessed; her husband also, and he praises her:

29 "Many women do noble things, but you (Mami) surpass them all."

—PROVERBS 31:28-29
NEW INTERNATIONAL VERSION (NIV)

Facebook Star is born

I STARTED POSTING PICTURES and statuses about my relationship with Mami, as soon as I became a member of Facebook. I quickly noticed that any post that had anything to do with Mami would get so much attention and a lot of "Likes". I loved it and she did too. I would show her the postings and explain to her what the "Likes" meant. I would also read the comments to her and she would smile. She called it "the Facebook". Many of our family and friends would also comment to her that they saw a picture of her on Facebook and that tickled her. She felt famous and popular.

I shared my postings of Mami without thinking about the impact it would have on others. It was just natural for me to share her because that is something I had done my entire life. Her smile was contagious and her beauty was radiating. My Mami was a beautiful woman and she did not look her age at all. She kept herself up and to be honest, she had no worries because we made sure of that. She lived her golden years in peace and just went with the flow. I knew Mami loved photographs because she took many of us growing up. So any opportunity I had to take selfies with her, she was willing. She loved my selfie-stick. She was always ready to cheese and pose for it and then she would ask if I was going to post it on "the Facebook". My response was always "of course".

Over the years, I came to find out by public comments or private messages how much people admired our relationship with Mami. They came to know her as "Mami" because that is how we posted her on Facebook. They looked forward to seeing pictures of her while she visited me in Georgia, when I went to Indiana to see her or when we took our adventurous trips together. They loved that beautiful smile and some actually admitted being jealous, but in a good way, because I had a relationship with Mami like they wanted to have with their mother and could not see that happening. Although, I enjoyed the admiration, I was saddened to know that what I had was not the norm. But, it helped me to understand even more how special Mami was. Therefore, I could not wait to post pictures or statuses of conversations that I had with her. My Facebook page is filled with pictures of Mami. She was my Facebook star. I was especially thrilled with the "Shared Memories" feature that Facebook introduced a few years ago. Because year after year, I can see all the great memories of Mami on my page. I continue to share memories of Mami, as they come up and at times it is difficult because it reopens the wound. But I try to focus on taking myself back to that moment when I was with her and how much I enjoyed the moment. While growing up in Panama, I would always hear people say "*recordar es vivir*", translated it means, "*to remember is to live*". I honestly believe that when I look back at the great memories on my Facebook page. Because I relive the moments and I feel alive again.

Upon arrival to Nassau, March 29th, 2017, one of the first things we did was take pictures. We took a family selfie and then we took pictures of Mami like the paparazzi. My extended brother Randy even joked about her posing for the pictures. I posted my picture of her with the Atlantis tower in the background. The caption for my post was "*Mami!!!! Anything for Her!*" and I meant that. I could not wait to post that particular picture because the smile on her face said it all. She was so happy to be in the Bahamas with her children, sister and grandchildren. Although it makes me sad to know that was the last picture of Mami alive that I posted that evening, it gives me joy to know that she was thrilled and happy to be there.

When I finally posted on my Facebook page what happened the following morning, the overwhelming response that followed was unexpected. My friends were so hurt because they had just seen the last posting with her big smile and a t-shirt that said *"I Can Do All Things"*. Now that I look back, that photograph was angelic and I believe God was preparing us and even my Facebook family and friends for the farewell. For the days and weeks to come, I found it hard to post anything that was not related to Mami. I wanted to honor her and thank everyone that reached out to support my family and me. I continued to post tributes to Mami. I had so many photos to choose from because we took photos so often with each other. It was hard to believe for many days that my Facebook star was gone. But, thanks to a Facebook comment, my star was immortalized on paper through this book. The suggestion of writing this book came from a Facebook comment from my cousin Luna F. Ramirez. The comment was from a posting about "Being a Godparent…", I felt the need that Sunday to share my examples of godparents in my life and where I got it from. I suddenly got many inbox messages encouraging me to write about Mami and share the recipe for success of mother/daughter relationship. I oftentimes hear people complain about Facebook and explain why they don't have an account. For me, Facebook is what you want it to be for you. For me it was a platform to share with my family and friends. I don't accept friend requests from strangers, so I feel safe posting personal things about my family. I plan to continue posting photos and memories of Mami for as long as I have a Facebook account. I want everyone to continue to know the importance of a mother/daughter relationship. I strongly believe it is the most important relationship any woman could ever have.

On May 4th, 2017 I received a phone call from a friend/colleague that recently left the company. His name is Naveen Suri. Naveen and I shared a love for traveling and photography and we became Facebook friends many years ago. I would admire his postings and would always comment that we needed to synch up our schedules to travel together. Naveen called to express his condolences and also his admiration for the tribute that I continued to post about Mami. During the conversation he expressed that her smile in her photos and my words made him feel like he should have met her. He said he felt a connection to her via my postings. I then proceeded to let him know that I was writing this book and his response was "brilliant". As our conversation continued, we both agreed that who we are is all based on our parents and what they instill in us. I asked about his job search and he expressed he was still in the process and he was looking forward to the change and I told him that change is good. Lastly I shared with him something that Abuela would always say to me, "every disappointment is for the best". He then said that I was raised by some great women and I totally agreed. We also agreed to meet up next time I was in New Jersey and I hung up with such comfort and pride knowing that Mami had touched someone via my Facebook page that she never met before.

I have so many postings of Mami and I on my Facebook page that it seems like a different memory comes up daily and I love it. I am enjoying and embracing the memories as they come. *#OnThisDay #Facebook #SocialMedia*

Angie Ford
NOVEMBER 2, 2015
Robin Gilliam and 99 others   26 Comments

👍 Like   💬 Comment   ➤ Share

Angie Ford posted a photo on Instagram — at ◦ **Atlantis Paradise Island - Nassau, Bahamas.**
March 29 at 7:49 PM · Instagram · 👥

Mami!!!! Anything for HER!!!😍😍👏👏

♥♥ 108   18 Comments

Angie Ford
NOVEMBER 1, 2014
Lisa A Rozzelle and 99 others   16 Comments

👍 Like   💬 Comment   ➤ Share

---

aford81266
Atlantis Paradise Island - Nas...

💬 Q ✈

liked by **dee_fab**, **purejoyessentials1** nd **35 others**
ford81266 Familia!!!!
iew all 6 comments
atasha.quintero nice...enjoy
hespiritualtraveler Sending love to

🏠   Q   ⊕   ♡   👤

I love you mama😍 See More

💬 41   7 Comments

👍 Like   💬 Comment   ➤ Share

📷 Edit
🎥 Edit

Angie Ford

📝 Post   👥 Edit Profile   ≡ Activity Log   ••• More

Peace is how we know we are following God's plan because God's plan always leads to peace!

💼 PMO and Operations Director at iconectiv

Happy 81st birthday to my lovely mami 👏👏👏 we love you so... See More

♥♥ 74   48 Comments

❤ Love   💬 Comment   ➤ Share

Comments   **Done**

Edwin Frias Frias
Saludos y abrazos a ti y a mi madrina
December 20, 2015 · Unlike · 👍 1 · Reply

  Angie Ford
  Igualmente para ti y tu familia
  December 20, 2015 · Like · Reply

  Edwin Frias Frias
  Gracias angie
  December 20, 2015 · Unlike · 👍 1 · Reply

  👤 Write a reply...

Edwin Frias Frias
Las dos hermosas
December 20, 2015 · Unlike · 👍 1 · Reply

Kinna Perry
Must Bonita😍
December 20, 2015 · Unlike · 👍 1 · Reply

Angie Ford

📷 Write a comment...   😊

👍 Like   💬 Comment   ➤ Share

Angie Ford
APRIL 12, 2015
Sterling Dunkley and 59 others   7 Comments

👍 Like   💬 Comment   ➤ Share

Saying So Long…

O N MARCH 30, 2017, our lives as Mami's daughters changed forever. But, we soon came to find out of the vast impact Mami had on so many and how their lives changed too. So many people hurt for and with us. They comforted us and felt like they had to do something to make us feel better and they did. It came in so many forms: cards, text messages, phone calls, food, flowers, money and just a tight hug. Because of Mami's faith and what she had instilled in us, we knew that Mami went straight to heaven. There was no doubt about that, we know she ascended immediately because she lived her life in preparation for that moment. She was always ready and at peace with everyone. Just a sweet and wonderful soul. She had no regrets and held no grudges.

Because Mami passed away in the Bahamas, we had the additional factor of getting her body back to the United States. So we had to deal with a local funeral home. I can't say that the process was smooth, because in the Bahamas nothing gets done on weekends and Mami died on a Thursday, we went on Friday to identify her and give a statement to the police. Fast forward to Monday, when work resumes they then started on the autopsy, which did not complete until Tuesday. By Wednesday, we had a flight to catch to return as our original flight back home from the vacation. We kept it like that because we needed to get back to handle the arrangement on this end. When we left, we found out that they had written her name wrong on a document and it was going to take a couple more days. But thankfully, we had made some connections locally through some dear friends and they helped to expedite the process. We had a funeral scheduled for Wednesday, April 12th, 2017 in Stone Mountain, Georgia and it was Holy week. By now, it was looking like Mami would not start her journey back to the Miami until Monday of Holy week and arrive in Atlanta on Tuesday of Holy week. My sisters and I made the decision to postpone the funeral until the Monday after Easter and that was the best decision we could have made for the entire family. But, we did not tell the funeral home in the Bahamas about it because we did not want them thinking they had more time to get Mami back to us. We all returned to the United States on Wednesday, as scheduled. My dear friends from my *Worship With Friends (WWF)* group converged on my home that Thursday. They wanted to lay eyes on me and bring dinner over. They came in and took over the kitchen. It was heartwarming and it did ease my pain. My family was still in town because they missed their connecting flights to New Orleans and Indianapolis. Therefore, they experienced this with me and I was glad to have them present.

Mami arrived in Atlanta on Tuesday of Holy week. That night was the first night since Mami had died that I was able to sleep through the night and it felt wonderful. My heart was at peace. We had already identified a funeral home in Decatur, Georgia to work with. It was Donald Trimble Mortuary. They picked up Mami and kept me informed of everything. The person I worked with directly to make the selections for Mami's services was Yolanda Harris, a soft spoken woman with 18 years of experience at Donald Trimble. I felt in good hands and I was. They say a funeral is the last thing you would ever do for your parent and we selected the best for Mami. We wanted her home-going celebration to be fit for the Queen that she was to us.

My baby sister Maritza and her family returned on Good Friday. I had gone to the DeKalb Farmers Market that Tuesday to get some fresh fish. I chose to get some whole red snapper to fry on Good Friday, as we did in Panama for many years during my childhood. I wanted the mood to be light and familiar. I invited my extended family and friends over for a fish fry that evening. We sat on the deck, fried the fish outdoors, ate some crawfish and drank a lot of beers. We had a good time, we laughed a lot and prepared for the arrival of more family the following days to come. By Saturday night, my family from Phoenix, Brooklyn, Philadelphia, New Orleans and Seattle had arrived. My baby sister Maritza, aka "The Contessa", prepared a jambalaya from scratch. Prior to that, we had spent the morning at Costco shopping for food and paper goods. Also that evening, the funeral home called to say Mami was ready for her first viewing. Only my baby sister Maritza, Tia Lois, Nia and Mae Ruth agreed to go. We went to see her and we were totally pleased. Mami's hair was perfect, like she had just left the salon and Shevella (my dear friend that had just passed a few weeks prior from cancer) had done her hair. She looked like she was sleeping and at peace. That made all of us feel better. We returned home to prepare for early Easter Sunday service at Ray of Hope Christian Church, my home church.

On Easter Sunday, we attended 7:30 AM service and then came back to cook breakfast. The Contessa was back in the kitchen making eggs, bacon, pancakes, fruit, coffee, etc. I had to eat quickly because I had another run to the airport. The Panama crew was scheduled to arrive at 11:04 AM. I tracked their flights and it was on time. We required two cars to go them and my brother-in-law followed me. We picked them up and brought them back to my home. The crowd was growing at my house and it felt good to be around my family. Once again, Mami had brought us all together. Within the Panama crew came her best friend, my Godmother Neva. She was cheerful upon arrival until it hit her that Mami was not sitting next to her on my couch like they usually would and it broke my heart to see her cry. I hugged her and laid her on my bed for her get some rest, as she had been traveling since 2:00 AM that morning. By the time I looked around, the North Carolina Johnsons had arrive, then the McQueens from New Jersey. My pool volleyball team members dropped by and brought so much food. The food was mostly homemade and prepared just for us and it was amazing. All the cooks in the family raved about it and asked to please get the recipes and I did. Only one more guest was pending to arrive and that was my sister's co-worker Cora, who was on the trip with us in the Bahamas. She is dear friend of the family and lives in Indianapolis. My extended brother offered to go pick her up from the airport. We sat on the deck and ate some more boiled crawfish and laugh as much as we could. We knew the following day would be difficult. I set up the backyard to have a movie on the green. We lit the fire pits and watched "Hidden Figures" under stars and enjoyed each other. My next door neighbors decided to join us. Then we came back inside and everyone went to their assigned quarters. I mentally prepared myself to wake up early and take a shower to get out of the way. I have four bathrooms and nineteen people in the house. Therefore, time was of the essence because the limos were scheduled to pick up at 10:15 AM the next morning.

We woke up and ate a continental breakfast in shifts. Everyone knew what time the limousines would arrive and that we would line up in front of my home to head for the viewing by 11:00 AM. Everyone was dressed and ready for when limousine and the funeral director arrived. We said a little prayer prior to our departure. I had the list of passengers for each car. We loaded up and followed the police escort to the church. My big sister Francie left before us because she was in charge of opening the church. This was her home church and the entire service was planned by her. She chose the musical selections for the mass and they were some of Mami's favorite songs. Mass was held in English, but all songs were in Spanish. Before leaving the Bahamas, I picked up a basket of shells from the market. I wanted to have a shell ceremony where everyone that viewed Mami would place a shell in the casket with her. It was beautiful because everyone that came in participated in the shell ceremony. I walked with my Godmother to place her shell on Mami and watched her place it on her heart. It gave me chills to see her do that. She wanted Mami to know that she would always live on in her heart. The programs prepared by the funeral home were beautiful. They were printed on an iridescent paper that made the picture collages stand out. I wanted the program to be a great keepsake and it was. I also wanted to have enough for everyone. We sent some to Panama and mailed to people who could not come to the services and they loved them.

The family and friends began to arrive. We met one of Mami's godbrother (Teddy) and godsister (Vinetta) for the first time at the funeral. They drove from Palm Coast, Florida. Mami had always spoken of them, but I had never physically met them. That was exciting for me. These were names I grew up hearing about. We also saw a dear friend of Mami's from New York. She had flown in the night before. Maritza's best friend, Lisa, flew in that same morning and came directly to the church. My friends in Georgia showed up and represented. Most had met Mami during the summers when she would come visit me. I also saw friends that I had not seen in quite some time and it warmed my heart to see and hug them. The message from Father JohnPaul was right on target. My nephews served that day by bringing the communion bread and wine to the altar. Prior to the funeral, I sent a text message to six of men in my family (Alan, Darrell, Ricky, Lucius, Ron and Randy) to ask them to be pallbearers because I wanted Mami to be in good and familiar hands. Everyone accepted and felt it was honor to be asked. I chose to speak about Mami at the end of the mass. I wanted to tell stories about Mami that many would not know. I wanted the mood to be light and funny. I got everyone to chuckle with my mischievous adventures as a child and how Mami reacted to some of the things I did. Some of the stories I have already shared in previous pages. It was the way we wanted to end the services. We wanted it to be a celebration of life and it was. My brother-in-law Alan, followed with the acknowledgements and thanked everyone for coming. He also shared some memories about Mami and the things he will miss the most about her.

The pallbearers got in place to put Mami back in the hearse and it was so touching to see the six men I had selected carrying her. We spent some time getting everyone back in their limousines and embracing with friends and family before we headed to Melwood cemetery. My cousin Martine and her husband Lucius headed home to prepare for the repast. Some of my close friends offered to cook some food and headed to the house to help Martine get the food going and set up for the arrival of our guests. We proceeded to the cemetery. The procession was long, the number cars was overwhelming to see. The police escort held us all together. The oncoming traffic stopped as we came along our route to the cemetery. They stopped to pay their respects and to allow for the police escort to maneuver to the following intersection. As we arrived at the cemetery, the police escort parked and got off their motorcycles to salute Mami as she passed by them in the hearse. It gave us goosebumps to see such an honorable show of respect. The tent was awaiting our arrival in the spot that my baby sister Maritza and I had selected as Mami's resting place. It was chosen because of the cherry blossom tree in the background. Father JohnPaul blessed the casket and said a few words. As he spoke the skies got really dark and a wind gust swept through the tent. I looked at my watch and it was almost 3 PM. It was biblical for those that know the significance of 3 PM on a Good Friday. Suddenly, the sky cleared and the sun came right back up. We were handed yellow roses as a keepsake or to put with Mami's casket. I chose to put mine with her. We took some time to take some family pictures and hug everyone that came to the emetery. We made sure everyone knew that we would be gathering at my home, thereafter. I had no worries about the preparations for the repast. I knew my cousin and my girls would take care of everything. When we got back to the house, sure enough everything was beautiful. We had so much food and it was delicious. My family and friends had done it again. They made it easy for me and my sisters. They served my plate and ensured that I ate. I changed clothing to be comfortable. I mingled with my guests and handed out prayer cards that I had made with Psalm 23 on the back of them, one of Mami's favorite verses in the bible and a beautiful picture of Mami on the front. We laughed, danced and had great conversation for the remainder of the night, until we retired at about 11 PM. It was a beautiful day and beautiful ceremony. We sent Mami off in style knowing that we would meet again. So long Mami…

Mami's funeral program read as follows:

Jean Arial Ford Alleyne

Sunrise: November 3, 1935
Sunset: March 30, 2017

Born Jean Arial to parents Mildred Folks and Castell Alleyne in Panama City, Panama where she lived most of her life. "Jeannie", as most people knew her, was a great mother, wife, grandmother, godmother, friend and neighbor. She was well known in her community, where she lived for over 40 years, for the way she always helped and supported the children and people in her community. She was a devout Catholic and member of Iglesia San Juan Bautista in Panama until she moved to Indiana in 2009 and became a member of St. Andrews in Indianapolis.

Jeannie lived life her way and on her terms. Always there to listen and to share whatever she had. Jeannie enjoyed traveling with her daughters and mother "Abuela" for many years. She was her eyes because "Abuela" was blind. They were two peas in a pod as they traveled together to visit family in the USA. She enjoyed trying new foods/drinks and just going with the flow. She also loved doing crossword puzzles, playing scrabble, watching Jeopardy and Wheel of Fortune. She was very good at all these word games and would win by any means necessary.

Her two biggest joys were seeing all three of her daughters graduate from Xavier University and becoming a grandmother. A role that she served extremely well. She helped with homework, made breakfast, picked up toys and cleaned up her grandson's rooms for many years. She made sure they got their daily blessings before they left the house. They were her pride and joy. They have grown into wonderful young men and she encouraged them to continue with their studies. She also enjoyed being a "Godmother" and took her role very seriously. She kept up with all her godchildren and was their confidant. She checked on them often and stayed connected with them regardless of where they lived. She wore her armor of God and her shield and she fought the good fight. She ran a great race and she won! Her job was well done and it is over. It is our hope that having been touched by her wisdom, we will all try to walk the same path that brings personal blessings, peace, love and gratitude that has been promised.

She is survived by her daughters Francella, Angelica and Maritza (spouse Alan), sisters Lois and Brenda (spouse Alfred), nieces Tamara, Tisha (spouse Reed) and nephew/godson Alfred, grandsons AJ and Jalen, great nephew Tyler, great niece Tatjana, godchildren (Tony, Xiomara, Tyra, Edwin, Karen, Gisela), best friends Neva, Yiniva, Elena Beverly and Janet, extended sons Ron and Randy, extended grandchildren Jasmine, Brycen, Emily and Gabriel and many other nieces, nephews, family members and friends in Panama and all over the United States.

That same week after the funeral, I went to order Mami's headstone from a local manufacturer and sat with a Hispanic man by the name of Mario. We spoke in Spanish and designed Mami's headstone. The final results is amazing. I paid a deposit of half of the total balance and the following day he called to say it was ready. I ran over there because it is located 15 minutes from my home. I was in amazement of the wonderful job he had done. Especially the way the inscription reads. It has "Mami" on it. That made me smile. The one word that I have uttered more than any other in my entire life. I paid him the remainder of my balance. The following week I met Mario at the cemetery to watch him install it. Mario took his time and did a great job. He was pleased with his own work and I was too. I took photos of him while he worked to share with my siblings and other family members. I wanted them to know that the final piece was in place. Mario washed it down and I placed some beautiful red and yellow flowers in the vases on each side of the headstone. It looked absolutely beautiful. My eyes got teary, but this time they were tears of joy because once again we had given Mami the best that we could give her. We wanted Mami to have her headstone in place prior to Mother's Day and we accomplished that. I went to visit her on Mother's Day after having breakfast to celebrate Jasmine's first Mother's Day. I wanted the day to be a celebration. I did not want to look at it as being my first Mother's day without Mami because it wasn't. Mami was always with me. I carry her in my heart and mind daily. I speak to her all the time. I ask her questions constantly. I ask her to watch over all of us and I know that she is doing just that. I can see her with that beautiful smile on her face, as always. She is forever my guardian angel.

I felt a strong need to go back to Panama soon after Mami's funeral and I did. I had a trip to Peru for work in mid-May, 2017 and decided to stop in Panama for three days to visit family and friends. Many family and friends were not able to make the funeral. Therefore, I felt obligated to go back and personally connect with them and also console them. I knew what Mami meant to each of them and how much they missed her. It was already hard for me to watch her leave and move to the United States and take her from her sisterhood. I was able to see some of my childhood friends and have dinner with them. I also went to our school to get Francie's graduation photo because she could not find her yearbook. While at our school, which has doubled in size, I saw many of my elementary teachers. Some of whom are now the administrators of the school. They all expressed their condolences and gave me a big hug. I spent most of my time with my Godmothers. They cooked for me and I ate so well while I was there. I felt right at home and I could feel Mami's presence with us the entire time. We laughed, cried and remembered all the good times with Mami. The weather was hot, humid and rainy. It was bitter sweet. But it was necessary and nevertheless home sweet home. It was hard to leave and as I said my goodbyes the tears just started flowing. I prayed to God to give me strength, as I departed and also asked for the opportunity to return by end of year to celebrate the holidays. Panama, my birthplace, my home forever. There is no place like home, no place like it. *#SoLong #Mami*

IN LOVING MEMORY

BELOVED MOTHER & GRANDMOTHER

JEAN FORD

"MAMI"

NOV. 3,
1935

MAR. 30,
2017

Grief

GRIEF IS DEFINED as suffering or hardship in the dictionary. It is what I am feeling as I write this chapter to complete this book. Although, the experience of writing has been cathartic and therapeutic, nevertheless the pain of losing Mami still prevails. I am told this will go on for many years and may never go away. I loved my Papi and I was very hurt when he died. But, the grief that I feel for Mami is so profound and unexplainable. It is the most painful experience I have ever had. On a daily basis, I feel like I am on a rollercoaster ride. I don't know what time of day the ride is going to start and I am not sure how long the ride will last. I just strap on and hang on until it subsides. In a day, I may have two, three or four rides. It is part of my new life and I am learning to cope with it. My hardest part of the day is when I get into my car. Since I work from home, Mami was always my go to person to call when I got in the car. We would chat until I reached my destination. For many days I would cry while I drove. But somehow, things started to change and it seemed like every time I would start to cry, my phone would ring. A family member or friend would just happen to call right at that moment and I would get distracted. I felt that Mami was sending these souls to rescue me and I would thank her. I also decided to talk to Mami while in the car because I can feel her presence with me. I talk to her all the time. I tell her good morning and good night every day. I kiss her pictures and I smile when I see her beautiful smile. I find ways to connect with her and feel her spirit throughout my day. I pray to her for protection.

My Soror LaShawn Ames added me to Facebook group titled "Sometimes I feel like a Motherless child". At first I was skeptical about being in the group. Because my grief was so fresh and I was not sure if I wanted to share it with people that I really didn't know. But I chose to remain and read some of the postings. I was added to the group right before Mother's Day of 2017. I found it helpful to know that there are so many other people like me in this world. I scrolled down and read some of the postings and I was able to find some comfort in knowing that I had Mami for so many years. Some people had lost their Mother's at very young ages. I had a lifetime with Mami and have no regrets. I gave her as much as I could because she deserved the best. Mami made many sacrifices for us and her entire family. She paid it forward and my sisters and I paid her back. The most common timeframe of the postings in this group is right before Mother's day. It seems to be the hardest of all holidays for the members of the group to cope with.

On Thursday, May 17th, 2017, a dear Sorority sister Sylvia Jones sent me a poem titled "Grief" by Gwen Flowers to my Facebook inbox. It was an eye-opener and it helped to release the weight I was carrying around trying to force myself to get through my grief. After reading it, I realized that there wasn't anything to do. That I just needed to accept my "new normal". From that day on, it became easier to cope on a daily basis. I began to see things differently. The words in this poem are so clear and profound. I immediately shared it on my Facebook and Instagram pages. I got so much feedback. One person wrote "I so needed this! Thank you!" Another wrote "That is so accurate". By the reaction that my friends on social media had, I knew this had opened their eyes also and that made me feel really good.

Grief

by Gwen Flowers

I had my own notion of grief.
I thought it was the sad time
that followed the death of someone you love.
And you had to push through it to get to the other side.
But I'm learning there is no other side.
There is no pushing through.
But rather, there is absorption.
Adjustment.
Acceptance.
And grief is not something you complete.
But rather, you endure.
Grief is not a task to finish and move on.
But an element of yourself, an alteration of your being.
A new way of seeing.
A new definition of self.

On July 23rd, my nephews and I traveled back to Indianapolis. They were returning from their summer vacation with me and I came to help my sister pack and clean Mami's room. We knew it was time and I knew she could not do it alone and should not have to. Because I work from home, it was easy for me to just tell my boss that I would be working from Indianapolis during that period of time. The entire week before my arrival, I kept dreaming of Mami. I think she was trying to ease my mind because anxiety had started to set in. I cried during the entire flight from Atlanta to Indianapolis. I was not ready to see her things and smell her in her room. I had spent so many nights in that room when I would come visit. I always slept with Mami and I slept like a baby. I cried so much as soon as I got into her bed and I allowed myself to. Because I knew it was part of the process. I had so much support from family and friends. I called my Tia Brenda in Phoenix and cried while expressing my anxiety to her. She managed to calm me down some. But, as soon as I hung up the phone with her, the tears started rolling again. I then called my Godmother Neva and she also made me feel better. By now, I was clear that it was ok to feel the way I was feeling and I just laid in Mami's bed and talked to her and strategize on how to start the clean up the following day. I then went through her well organized photo system. Mami had the best system with photos of the entire family. Not only photos, she has our certificates, diplomas, hand-made cards, report cards, etc. in these cases. The photos are stored by categories of events and people. Each in its on plastic case. It was bitter sweet. I laughed and cried all at the same time, as I went through each individual case within the big cases. I shared some of the photos of Mami as an adolescent on my Facebook page. A friend commented on that specific photo that she had been looking at for hours and could not figure out who Mami reminded her of and it finally hit her that she looked like Nia Long. As soon as I read that comment, I totally agreed, because I was wondering who also. I kept looking at it saying to myself that she reminded me of someone. I continued to share more photos, as I found them. It was cleansing to share these with my family and friends and read all the comments from them.

On Monday, July 24th, I got up a little later than usual. My sister Maritza came in to say she was headed to work and I shared my plan to go buy some boxes and start packing things up. I proceeded with my plan by 10 AM that morning. Went to Walmart and bought the boxes, tape and markers to label the boxes. I then, went through all the drawers in the dresser, armoire, night table and desk. I started to put the boxes together and began loading them up. By 5PM my sister came home from work and began cooking. I was wearing some of Mami's joggers at this point and I felt comfortable. We even laughed about that too. When Maritza was done cooking she joined me in Mami's room to continue the process and we agreed on what to pack and what to discard. Mami had so many clothes, shoes, photos and purses. We got through all her drawers and decided what to donate to the thrift shop at Mami's church. It was boxed up and ready to go the following day. We also tackled her jewelry and her grandsons came in decided what they wanted to keep and the rest we kept to share with family and some we also donated to her church. All photos were kept as is because they were already so well organized. My big sister Francie asked me to bring back pictures of herself and that was so easy. Because I just had to look for the case with her photos and put it aside in my luggage. Maritza and I decided to call it quits by around 9PM and continue the following day. We then went for a walk around the neighborhood with "Sochi", the family dog. When we returned, I took a shower, said my prayers, spoke to Mami for a few minutes and slept like a baby in her bed.

On Tuesday, July 25th, I woke up early to continue my task, as my sister Maritza went to work. She had five patients to see that day. I began with the closet, which was the last thing we had to do. My Godmother Neva had already requested Mami's blazers and jackets. Therefore, I pulled those out first, created a box to mail back to Georgia and pack in December when we head down to Panama for the Holidays to see her and the rest of the family. I continued surveying the contents of the closet in advance of my sister's arrival from work and began separating what I thought we would give to our family in Panama and what would go to Mami's church. My sister Maritza joined me that evening to complete our task of tackling the closet and we did. It was such a relief to be able to reach our goal. The rest of the evening was spent with our family friend Cora, who was with us in the Bahamas when Mami transitioned. My brother-in-law Alan grilled and we had a tasty meal and enjoyed each other's company. The following day we loaded up my nephew's SUV and took the donations to St. Andrews Church. But unfortunately, the thrift shop at the church was no longer in operations. Therefore, Sister Pam recommended that we donate the items to Mission 27 downtown Indianapolis. Therefore, we headed there to drop off the boxes. It was a gratifying feeling because we knew that is what Mami would have wanted us to do. Just knowing that someone in need would benefit from all those beautiful clothes, shoes and purses brought a big smile to my face.

Wherever a beautiful soul has been, there is a trail of beautiful memories. As a freelance photographer, I have so many pictures of Mami and I am so glad. The cover photo, I took as we celebrated her 80th birthday in Rome and dined across from the Coliseum. We made a toast to life and one well lived. I had a blast compiling the collage on the following pages. It brought back so many great memories. It made me smile just to see her smile in these photographs. Mami was such a beautiful woman. She had silky fine hair. Growing up, I would always stare at her and be so proud to be her daughter. I would always hear people whisper about her beauty. I am a product of this woman. I am her legacy and she will live on through me, for as long as I live. ***#Mami #BeautifulSoul #ForeverLoved***

I Love My Family

"In the end, just three things matter: How well we have lived. How well we have loved. How well we have learned to let go."

– JACK KORNFIELD

About The Author

Angelica "Angie" Ford was born and raised in Panama City, Panama in 1966. She moved to the United States to go to college in 1985 on a basketball scholarship. She obtained a Bachelor of Science degree in Mathematics and Computer Science from Xavier University of Louisiana in New Orleans in December, 1988. She then went on to get her Master's degree in Computer Science at  Howard University in Washington, DC in 1990. In 1996, she was nominated for the "Black Engineer of the Year Award" sponsored by Council of Engineering Deans of HBCU, Mobil Corporation and U.S. Black Engineer Magazine. That same year she was featured in the Black Collegian Magazine, as an outstanding engineer in the field of telecommunications. Angie is also a member of Zeta Phi Rho chapter Alpha Kappa Mu Honor Society from Xavier University.

Angie is currently the Director of PMO/Operations for Latin America at iconectiv. She has been working in software development for the telecommunications industry since she left college in 1988. She has worked and lived abroad in Argentina, Chile, India, Mexico, Peru and Thailand. She is a member of the prestigious Delta Sigma Theta Sorority, Inc. and the founder of DOWAP (Dining Out With A Purpose). She has dedicated her personal life to giving back to her community and helping others. Angie enjoys traveling and seeing the world. Among other of her hobbies is cycling, hiking, photography and writing. She took up writing a few years ago after taking several life changing trips and work assignments abroad as an expat. In order to describe her photographs, she decided to tell short stories about her travel experiences. This evolved into a love for expressing herself through words and was the seed for writing this book about her beautiful Mami.

Angie hopes that by sharing her experience of her relationship with Mami she will help anyone to forge strong bonds not only with their Mother, but with anyone they have an opportunity to spend significant time with.

Francella A. Ford
Stone Mountain, Georgia

Maritza Ford-Johnson
Indianapolis, IN

Printed in the USA
CPSIA information can be obtained
at www.ICGtesting.com
LVHW061115161023
761155LV00036B/1225/J